IN THE

DAYS

OF THE

PHARAOHS

IN THE

DAYS

OF THE

PHARAOHS

A Look at Ancient Egypt

by **Milton Meltzer**

SCHOLASTIC INC.

New York Toronto London Auckland Sydney
Mexico City New Delhi Hong Kong Buenos Aires

Cover and inside illustrations by Gary Overacre
Cover and interior design by Molly Heron

Photographs ©: Ancient Art & Architecture Collection Ltd./Ronald Sheridan: 122; Ancient
Egypt Picture Library/Robert Partridge: 118, 133 left (British Museum, London, UK), 112
bottom (Musee du Louvre, Paris), 33 bottom, 37 top, 114; Art Resource, NY: 34 bottom, 107
top (Borromeo), 39 bottom (Giraudon), 2, 23, 28, 32, 33 top, 37 bottom, 40, 68, 74, 77, 86, 106
bottom, 107 bottom, 142 (Erich Lessing), 35 bottom, 133 right (Scala), 106 top (SEF), 51 (Werner
Forman Archive), 112 top (Werner Forman Archive/British Museum, London), 108 bottom
(Werner Forman Archive/Musee du Louvre, Paris), 108 top (Werner Forman Archive/The
Egyptian Museum, Cairo), 98, 126; Bridgeman Art Library International Ltd., London/New
York: 38 (Ancient Art and Architecture Collection LTD/British Museum, London, UK), 83, 91
(Ashmolean Museum, Oxford, UK), 88 (British Museum, London, UK); Corbis-
Bettmann/Roger Wood: 36; Mary Evans Picture Library: 62, 144; National Geographic Image
Collection/Kenneth Garrett: 12, 18; Photo Researchers, NY: 34 top (Brian Blake), 35 top (James
Hanley), 92 (Christian Jegou/Publiphoto), 110 (Fred Maroon); Superstock, Inc.: 140 (Egyptian
National Museum, Cairo, Egypt/ET Archive), 44 (Explorer, Paris), 80, 105, 109 (Silvio Fiore),
25, 132, (Giraudon, Paris), 128, 134 (Musee du Louvre, Paris), 113 (Robert Thom), 20, 39 top,
56, 100, 111 top, 120, 136; The Art Archive/Jacqueline Hyde: 111 bottom (British Museum), 17
(Egyptian Museum Turin).

ISBN 0-531-18667-9

12 11 10 9 8 7 6 5 4 3 2 1   2 3 4 5 6 7/0

Printed in the U.S.A.   23

First Scholastic paperback printing, November 2002

CONTENTS

IN THE

DAYS

OF THE

PHARAOHS

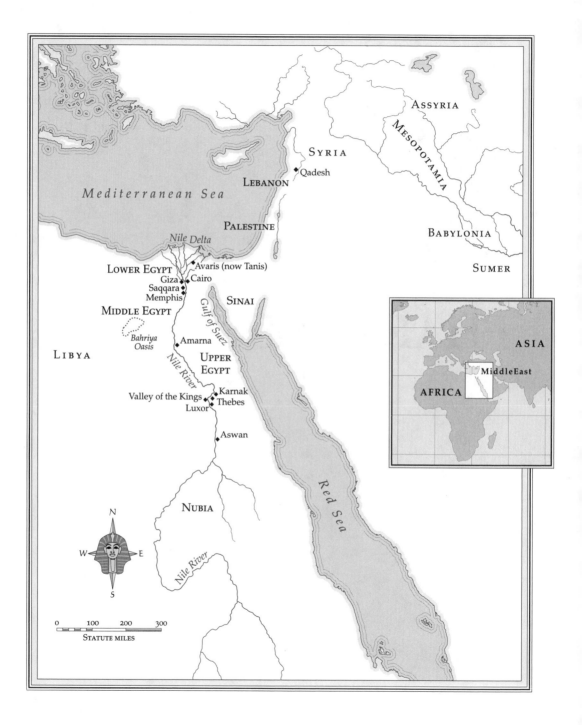

ASSYRIA

SYRIA

MESOPOTAMIA

LEBANON ◆ Qadesh

Mediterranean Sea

PALESTINE

BABYLONIA

Nile Delta

SUMER

LOWER EGYPT ◆ Avaris (now Tanis)

Giza ◆◆ Cairo
Saqqara ◆
Memphis

SINAI

MIDDLE EGYPT

*Bahriya
Oasis*

◆ Amarna

LIBYA

Gulf of Suez

UPPER
EGYPT

Nile River

Valley of the Kings ◆◆ Karnak
Luxor ◆ Thebes

◆ Aswan

Red Sea

N

W   E

S

NUBIA

Nile River

0   100   200   300
STATUTE MILES

ASIA

MiddleEast

AFRICA

INTRODUCTION

This is a story of buried treasure, of precious stones and artifacts found in tombs lost to history long ago. But even more exciting than these costly finds is another discovery. It is the unique knowledge brought to us by every fragment unearthed from the ancient sites. We recover, from deep within the earth, a part of human history we never knew was there. We learn of the birth of civilization, of the earliest cities ever built, and of the people who lived in them, of their thoughts, their achievements, their loves, their tragedies, their art, and their religion . . . five thousand years ago when their world was new.

It is the story of ancient Egypt, "the oldest and most splendid of all Eastern civilizations," says one scholar. The kingdom of the pharaohs began more than five thousand years ago, and has continued as a distinct political entity for seven thousand years. (Compare that span of time to the life of the United States of America, a nation born a little more than two hundred years ago.)

Did ancient Egypt never change in these millennia? That is a common view, but not an accurate one. Change did take place, certainly more slowly than in our hectic world of today, where change occurs with such rapid and often confusing speed. In many fields of knowledge—agriculture, astronomy, mathematics, medicine, philosophy, art, literature, and political science—the Egyptians made advances that preceded ours by thousands of years.

On the map, the rectangular shape of Egypt is set on the northeast edge of Africa. It is almost 1 1/2 times the size of Texas. The Mediterranean Sea is on the north, the Gulf of Suez and the Red Sea on the east, and the desert on the south and west, a part of the vast Sahara.

The vertical blue line running south to north on the east side of the country is the Nile River. It's the only major river in the world that flows from south to north. It draws its water from the large lakes of East Africa and the Ethiopian highlands as well as the equatorial rainfall. The river's two main tributaries, the White Nile and the Blue Nile, join together near what is now Khartoum.

The Nile—4,160 miles (6,693 km) long, the longest river in

the world—has always been at the heart of Egyptian life. The ancient Egyptians called their country *Kemet*, meaning "the Black Land," because of the rich mud which countless floodings have spread over the land. And the desert was called *Daghret*, meaning the Red Land.

But most of ancient Egypt's 1 million people—a very rough estimate—were crowded into a cultivated region of some 12,500 square miles (32,375 square kilometers). That is only about 3 percent of Egypt's total area. The rest is desert. Within Egypt, the Nile runs downstream from Aswan to the Mediterranean Sea. About 600 miles (966 km) of it belongs to the narrow river valley.

You could call the green valley of the Nile the Earth's greatest oasis. It cradled the civilization of Egypt.

Scientists hope that Egyptian mummies will help unravel some of the mysteries of ancient times.

CHAPTER ONE

HOW WE KNOW
WHAT WE KNOW

Who were the Egyptian people who created the world's first nation-state? We don't know. Scientists examining tissue samples from Egyptian mummies are finding traces of DNA in four-thousand-year-old bodies. "If enough DNA can be extracted and cloned," says one report, "we may be able to settle the question of the true origins of the Egyptians. No one really knows from where they first entered the Nile basin."

Some have claimed that the ancient Egyptians were black Africans. However, according to the anthropologist Brian M. Fagan, "There is no evidence that ancient Egypt was a black

African civilization as some scholars have claimed, even if there was constant interaction between the land of the pharaohs and Nubia . . . for more than 3,000 years." But Egypt's civilization, he emphasizes, "was nourished by constant contacts with black African civilizations up the Nile."

Ancient Egypt was influenced by many groups of people over its long history. The country was a crossroads over which many peoples traveled. As a result, scholars believe that several groups were absorbed into the native population, such as Berber, Bedouin, Semitic, Greek, and Levantine.

This leads us to the question: How do we know what we know about ancient Egypt? Much of our information comes from records, chronicles, biographies, stories, and poems left behind by this ancient civilization. For instance, from a history text of the ancient land by an Egyptian priest, we gained a better understanding of who ruled when, and learned that the history of ancient times could be divided into thirty dynasties.

However, inquiry—the essential element in studying history—was lacking in these accounts. No one attempted to reconstruct, by personal investigation, any aspects of Egypt's past. This type of investigation would not occur until an outsider tried to write about Egypt's history. He was Herodotus, the "Father of History," a Greek of the fifth century B.C., who traveled widely in the Middle East seeking information. He visited Egypt, interviewed people, and wrote about its past, its manners and customs, its religion, its pyramids, and some of the pharaohs. He inquired not only about the facts, but particularly about their meaning. Modern research tells us, however, that he wasn't too accurate or thorough.

Not until the nineteenth century were sources uncovered to help the world understand ancient Egypt. The most important hunt for sources, often buried, has been carried out by archaeologists. They search for the material remains left by our prehistoric and historic forbearers. On the basis of what they find, combined with other kinds of information, archaeologists reconstruct the human behavior and events of the past.

It's important to approach archaeological evidence with caution, though. It is often "impossible to infer social arrangements, institutions, attitudes, or beliefs from material artifacts alone," according to the classical scholar M. I. Finley. The artifacts are important data for history, but they do not reveal the thinking, the conventions, or the values they represent. For that, some literary evidence is needed.

It has become clear, too, that the particular interests of the archaeologist who does the excavation influence what he or she finds, and influence what he or she records even more so. For instance, suppose an archaeologist who specializes in studying daily life in ancient Egypt has found a tomb. That person may focus on any artifacts or any artwork related to his or her specialty, rather than study the details on a coffin. For example, some five people witnessed the opening of a tomb in the Valley of the Kings in the early 1900s. All wrote about it, no two agreed about what they saw.

The three principal sources of what we know are written, monumental, and artistic. To take the written first: The ancient

Egyptian writing system is one of the oldest in the world—probably only the Sumerian is older. It came into being before 3000 B.C., and remained in use until about the eleventh century A.D., when Arabic replaced it.

The written material is enormous, much of it religious, whether cultic (related to religious worship or ritual) or funerary (related to funeral practices). Besides religious writings, archaeologists have found important autobiographical texts in the tombs of non-royal individuals. Furthermore, thousands of non-religious documents have been preserved, due to Egypt's hot, dry climate or through being buried in sand. Much of this written evidence appears on papyri. Papyrus, a reed-like plant harvested in swampy land, was crafted for many uses, including a writing surface.

Written evidence is also found on ostraca—pieces of broken pottery or flakes of limestone, inscribed with written messages. And a sizable body of literature is recorded on papyri as well as everyday documents such as letters, wills, contracts, police reports, business accounts, and administrative reports. The cheaper ostraca were used for making lists, receipts, school exercises, and just plain scribbling.

Archaeologists have found a wealth of sources of written, monumental, and artistic information in the excavated tombs. The Egyptians decorated the walls of their tombs with naturalistic murals in brilliant colors. Many of the reliefs carved or painted on tomb or temple walls are religious in nature. But scenes from the family life of the dead are also depicted. Because the walls were made of stone, they have survived.

Researchers believe that this ostracon is some form of business record of a prince.

Statues found in tombs suggest the styles of dress, hair, and adornment worn by these ancient people. Portraits of kings are extremely rare, and the style of the pharaoh's features tells us what the pharaoh liked, not what he actually looked like.

Many items buried in the tombs were made for the burial chamber, but there were also objects used in daily life—sometimes the actual objects and sometimes models of them. Only the king, the nobles, and the wealthy could afford tombs; the vast majority of Egyptians were buried in graves in the desert

An anthropologist removes beads from a mummy before studying the body more closely.

sand. These too, however, may contain such ordinary possessions as tools, weapons, and pots.

The bodies of the dead, whether rich or poor, are an invaluable source of information. The upper classes were preserved by mummification. This practice began around 2600 B.C. and continued into the fourth century A.D. The bodies of the poorer classes too, while buried in simple graves, underwent a natural mummification because of the dry climate.

Despite the many sources that help bring ancient Egypt to life, it must be remembered that the information is by no means complete. The scholars often run into gaps in the record. In the Nile Delta region, few finds have been made, either because tombs and ruins remain buried or have been destroyed by the high water levels. Yet, up to five hundred decorated tombs have been found—from Giza to Aswan—made during five centuries of the Old Kingdom. Research is ongoing. Future excavations will surely yield new evidence. New findings will probably mean reevaluation of previously accepted opinions.

This photograph shows the Nile River in Aswan, Egypt.

CHAPTER TWO

THE NILE—
RIVER OF LIFE

In ancient times, the Nile was never more than a few miles wide, except in the 160-mile (257-km)-wide Delta region. The annual floods of the river shaped Egypt's economy and the rhythm of life along its banks. Before they learned to farm, prehistoric people caught or collected what food nature happened to provide. Like all the people on Earth, the Egyptians fed themselves by hunting wild animals, gathering wild plants, and fishing.

It was not an easy life and it was short. Most people lived in bands, tiny groups of five to eighty people, closely related by birth or marriage. While the men in the band hunted, the women collected whatever food was nearby. Their task required endless patience and persistence. Food-gathering was just as important as hunting, which was not always successful. Everyone depended on what the women gathered.

The invention of farming made life less hard. Archaeologists believe that farming began about 10,000 years ago, independently in several parts of the world. Egypt was not among the first civilizations to farm. Egypt raised its own crops in the sixth or early fifth century B.C. Another nearby civilization was one of the early innovators of agriculture, however. Sumer was located in the Tigris and Euphrates River Valleys in what is now Iraq. It is possible that the people of the Nile came into contact with the Sumerians, and learned from them how to raise some of the same domestic plants, such as wheat and barley. Most important, Egyptians learned how to grow more than they needed for daily consumption.

Farming gradually took root in the beds of mud deposited higher and higher each year along the Nile. Improved production of a variety of foods led to the rise of civilization. Farmers had to stay close to their fields and animals, living in fixed communities. When the people stayed in one place, they could store the food surplus and protect it. The production of food no longer required everyone's labor. Farming allowed some people to focus on other occupations.

Some Egyptians became priests, scribes, and artisans. Others rose to the top of their communities and became chieftains by inheriting leadership, or winning it by their strength

Farming helped the civilization of ancient Egypt to flourish.

and achievements. In the larger communities, the population became more stratified—the society began to develop different classes or social levels. As these communities grew ever more complex, they may have invaded neighbors to add to their territory, as some scholars have suggested. Other experts think that communities united as a result of trade.

Egyptian civilization depended almost entirely on irrigated agriculture. As a result of heavy rains in tropical regions far to the south of Egypt, the Nile flooded from June to September. About two weeks before the river reached its full height at Cairo, near the end of September, the floodwaters began to fall.

Not until April did they sink to their lowest level throughout the country.

The Nile's gift to Egypt was water and silt, a material made up of minerals found on the riverbed. This fertile silt from the highlands of Ethiopia added nutrients to the land and nourished Egypt's crops. As far back as 5200 B.C., Egypt's early farmers had learned to tame the floods to water the banks of the river. When a flood receded, the farmers would cast their seeds in the mud. To better control their water supply, farmers built dikes across their plots of ground to create basins. The basins held enough water to soak into the soil so that it could sustain the roots of crops during the growing season. At those times when too much water flooded in, the farmers simply broke their dikes to let the water run out.

The majority of the people were farmers. During late summer, the flooding of the Nile brought a temporary halt in farming, however. Peasant labor was then directed to building and handicrafts. Plowing the land and sowing the seeds required strenuous labor, as did the digging of canals and dikes and their repair. Harvest time made another call on hard labor.

As a way of life, farming was not admired. The rich had only contempt for such a sweaty and unprofitable occupation. Educated people praised their own work while contrasting it with the misery of farming. Yet it was the farmer who made Egypt—if not himself—wealthy. A sizable part of what a farmer produced was taken by the tax collectors.

On the fertile soil of the Nile Valley, farmers raised grains and flax—a plant used to make linen cloth. The vegetables

A painting found in the Valley of the Kings shows farmers harvesting grapes.

included beans, lentils, cucumbers, leeks, and onions. The fruits included dates, figs, and grapes. Flowers were grown too. Farmers raised domestic animals, such as African cattle (the Egyptians loved beef), sheep, goats, pigs, and donkeys. Flocks of geese and ducks were common. Later, during late Hyksos time when foreigners ruled the land, the Egyptians also had horses.

A farmer did not always own the land he worked. But whether he worked on royal land, fields owned by temples, or the estate of some great landlord, it was all the same to him.

His wages were paid in kind. Money had not yet been invented. What he got for his labor was grain and oil.

Sometimes, as in the twelfth century B.C., when the Nile failed more often than usual, life was harsh. Peasant families wavered between poverty and destitution. But despite their difficult situation, the peasants were expected to set aside some of their grain for taxes. They were not taxed on how much they actually harvested, but on how much the tax collector said they should have harvested. The tax collector calculated, on the basis of how high the Nile flooded that year, how much grain could be grown per acre. If the farmer's fields didn't yield what was predicted, he still had to pay that full share of taxes. And if he fell behind in his taxes, the collector beat him viciously.

Taxation was not the only burden for the peasant. At any time, he could be forced to work at specific tasks, such as the erection of pyramids and temples, the construction and maintenance of roads, irrigation canals, and dikes. He could be called to army duty or work in mines and quarries when extra manpower was needed. When he was employed on state projects, the state provided food for the peasant and his family.

Sometimes, when living conditions were more than a man could bear, peasants, in utter despair, would lay down their tools, leave their families, homes, and fields, and run away. Some runaways hid in the swamps and the desert or tramped from village to village begging for food. Others joined roving bands of robbers and preyed on isolated villages and wayfarers.

As Egyptian society developed, markets sprang up. There, people could meet to sell their products and buy goods from others. A peasant, for instance, might come to market to sell dried fish or a basket his wife had woven, taking linen and clothing in exchange. No one in an official position had yet thought of cutting and stamping round pieces of metal of an exactly controlled and uniform weight that would be accepted as a system of valuing produce and manufactured articles.

The peasantry had no power, and few could ever hope to rise above their lowly class in life. Few pharaohs showed a real interest in doing anything to improve the farmer's life or protect his interests. The royalty and the upper classes held most of the privileges and power in this ancient society. Democracy was a long way off for any part of the world.

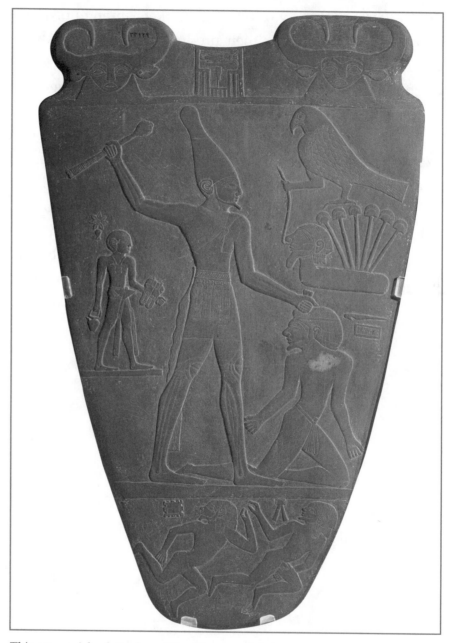

This ceremonial palette shows King Narmer subduing an enemy in his efforts to unify Egypt. The crown he wears represents Upper Egypt.

CHAPTER THREE

PHARAOHS, LAWS, AND GOVERNMENT

Egypt did not always have a king. Back around 4000 B.C., before the Egyptian dynasties were established, the Nile Valley was dotted with villages—the centers of farming life. Some scholars assume that one of the many local chieftains must have taken control of Upper Egypt, and another of Lower Egypt, and become their kings. The scholars speculate that, around 3200 B.C. one of these kings, called Narmer, unified the independent states of north and south Egypt and made himself the first pharaoh. The word *pharaoh* meant "great house." It was a way of referring to the royal palace in the New

Kingdom; the term soon began to be used to refer to the king himself.

For the next three thousand years, Egypt would be ruled by kings who had absolute power. The people considered them to be gods on Earth, in complete control of every aspect of life. The king was revered not only as a leader, but as the embodiment of Egypt itself.

Until Narmer took the throne, the country had been rather isolated, partly because of its geographic position. No military records have been found for the few centuries after Narmer, but a slate slab known as the Palette of King Narmer shows the king preparing to sacrifice an enemy. Narmer may have led troops up into southern Palestine or traded goods outside of his own country. But no national professional army was created until the New Kingdom (1550 to 1070 B.C.).

The king was the head of state. He was in charge of the government and the army, and he was also the priest of every temple. He embodied the Egyptian concept of *ma'at*, which means "order" or "justice." The people knew the king could be killed, or would die, but his essence was regarded as divine and immortal. He was a divine being, born of a god. The idea of divine kingship developed over a long span of time with the construction of immense tombs and temples and pyramids, and a complex ritual. The bas-reliefs in temples depict kings being welcomed into the world of the gods as one of their own, speaking to the gods as equals. It all helped create in the people's minds the belief in the reality of the immortal kingship of the pharaoh.

It is hard to construct an accurate and complete chronological list of all the pharaohs who reigned over three millennia and more. But the names of a great many kings and the sequence in which they reigned are known. The information is gleaned from tombs and temples, together with other sources. In periods of great national turmoil when central control was lost, civil war broke out, or foreigners occupied the country, records were damaged or disappeared. And some rulers removed from all records the names of those kings they wanted to be forgotten.

The first attempt to chronicle the kings of Egypt, using ancient sources, was made around 300 B.C. by Manetho, an Egyptian priest and scholar. He divided the list into thirty dynasties. Modern historians divide ancient Egyptian history into three kingdoms—Old, Middle, and New—separated by three Intermediate Periods. Another list of about three hundred kings, was found on a papyrus from about 1300 B.C.

It's not easy to figure out the timescale of this civilization. The calendar year as we know it did not yet exist. The Egyptians measured time according to the reign of each king. A new year began with the reign of each king and ended with his death. In the three Intermediate Periods, there were rival kings using their own dating systems. For other periods, no records have survived.

The oldest sons of the pharaohs were destined for the throne and trained from childhood to prepare to rule in the New Kingdom. Much stress was placed on building body strength because a king's time was often taken up with war. In

This stone carving shows Rameses III destroying his enemies with his club.

those days, kings rode at the head of their army. They did not stay safely behind, issuing orders from afar to the commanders.

The records show kings bragging about their physical power. One cited his skill in archery; he could pierce a copper plate with his arrows. At the royal stables, princes learned to ride horses, to break wild horses, and to test their own endurance in long footraces. In hunting expeditions beyond their own land, the royals matched themselves against wild beasts. One king, it is said, boldly took on the biggest elephant in a herd of 120 animals in the Euphrates Valley, placing himself in great danger. At home, they hunted lions, wild bulls, and antelope.

A peasant couple ploughs their field in this wall painting from a tomb found in Thebes.

Most of the peasants worked as farmers and spent their lives tending their crops along the Nile River.

Ancient Egyptians hunted pigeons, geese, ducks, and quails for food. This wall painting depicts a man hunting for birds in a papyrus swamp.

Animals, such as gazelles, were also an important source of food for the Egyptians.

This papyrus shows one of the many boats the Egyptians used to travel on the Nile River.

Hunting and fishing were popular sports for royalty and the upper classes. This statue shows King Tutankhamun standing on a boat made of papyrus stems and holding a harpoon.

Unlike modern warfare, pharaohs often rode ahead of their troops and became actively involved in battles.

Egyptian soldiers carried long shields and spears as shown in this painting from a temple for Queen Hatshepsut.

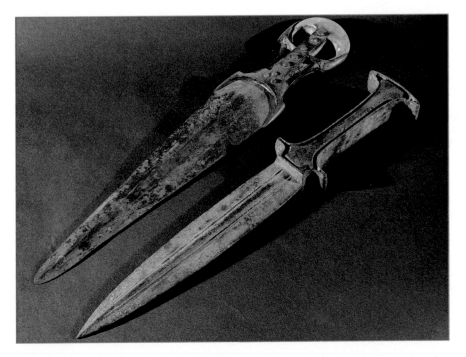

The dagger on the left is from the Middle Kingdom and is made of copper. After the Hyksos introduced the Egyptians to bronze, they were able to make more durable weapons, such as the bronze dagger from the New Kingdom on the right.

The top of this papyrus shows peasants dragging building blocks. They provided the labor necessary to create some of Egypt's most lasting landmarks.

The three large pyramids in this photograph were built during the Fourth Dynasty. The largest one by King Khufu stretches across 13 acres (5 hectares) of desert.

Four colossi, or statues, of Rameses II stand by the door of his great temple in Abu, Egypt.

From this Eighteenth Dynasty wall painting, it is possible to see artisans at work, making vases and other objects.

In the early dynasties, the king's sons and close relatives served him as counsel and aides. But as the Middle Kingdom began, a *vizier*, or prime minister, from outside the royal family might be appointed. The capital of the land was then in the north, at Memphis.

The country was divided into provinces or districts called *nomes*, administered by *nomarchs*, or governors. That post eventually became hereditary, passed on from father to son. The king, in principle, owned all the land. He rewarded his ministers or other worthy subjects deserving it with gifts of tax-free land. This created a wealthy landed gentry, something like the lords in a feudal society.

The work of the vizier was so great that the office was sometimes shared by two men. Each administered one section of the country, or controlled one particular function. The viziers oversaw agriculture, irrigation, justice, police, state grain supplies, finance and taxation, and construction projects. Men below them headed each of these institutions. To further disperse the administrative tasks, *nomes* or provinces were established to ease the burden on the central authority. But this placed power in the hands of the provincial governors, and some were tempted to set themselves up as independent rulers.

Managing income and expenses is always a vital part of any government, and the treasury was central to Egypt's administration. The vizier controlled it. He collected taxes, and redistributed raw materials and revenues to meet the needs of the pharaohs and the government, including such massive construction work as the pyramids.

The viziers also were responsible for seeing that justice was done and that public order was maintained—never an easy job in any society. In every period of Egypt's history, even under the best kings, crimes of all kinds and abuses of power occurred. Organized gangs looted temples and tombs where vast treasures were kept. From the Old Kingdom on, people were warned by highly visible engraved signs not to damage or steal anything, for their misdeed would be punished: "May the crocodile attack him in the water and the serpent on land . . . God himself will punish him."

The arm of the law—from vizier to judge to the humblest police officer—was an object of awe to the workers and

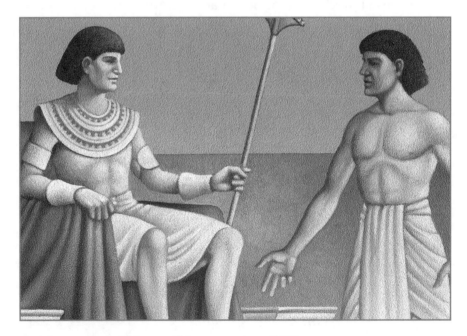

A vizier oversees a trial, one of his many responsibilities.

peasants. The arrival of an officer often foreshadowed a beating or the confiscation of property. Fear of punishment by the law—or by the gods after death—protected temples and tombs, so long as an honest and vigilant police force was on guard. But during intervals of unrest and upheaval, says archaeologist Pierre Montet, "the scribes, the tax collectors, and the minor bureaucracy hideously oppressed the poor and robbed the people and the king alike. When anyone appealed to justice, those whose business it was to protect the taxpayer took bribes to acquit the guilty and to condemn the innocent victim who could not afford to purchase their favor."

Magistrates convicted of such abuse had their noses cut off and were sent to a horrible kind of prison camp. Officials caught in wrongdoing might get one or two hundred blows from a club, have to restore what they had stolen, and pay a hundred times that value by way of penalties and interest. Sometimes the guilty would have their noses and ears cropped too, and assigned to a temple as laborers.

The robbing of tombs, whether of kings or commoners, was sometimes done by minor temple officials. The gang of thieves might include priests and scribes. In trials of suspected criminals, the judges requested the names of co-conspirators. If the prisoner hesitated to give names, he might be beaten, again and again, until the court was satisfied he had told all. Those who were convicted faced various punishments, from banishment abroad to labor in mines or quarries, to being tied to a stake, and perhaps left there to die. Only rarely, according to scholars, was a prisoner released.

Ancient Egyptians plunged into a time of conflict and discord after the end of the Old Kingdom.

CHAPTER FOUR

WARS AND WARRIORS

No one knows why the Old Kingdom ended. After the incredibly long reign of Pepi II, the country entered what historians call the First Intermediate Period (2200–2060 B.C.). This First Intermediate Period, coming between the Old Kingdom and the Middle Kingdom, lasted for well over a century. Records of some of the kings have been found. Some civil wars broke out as local rulers struggled for power. Rioters destroyed tombs, organized work stoppages, and attacked government offices. Faith in religion declined, and the authority of the kings faded. From the East came infiltrators called "Asians."

Egypt did not have a professional army until after the First Intermediate Period. That chaotic time, when unruly provincial nobles were killing one another, taught the rulers a grave lesson. A large-scale professional army was essential to keep order at home and to conquer other territories. Its members were largely drawn from the middle class. Armed battalions were also used to protect expeditions to mine sand quarries.

Up to this time, standing armies were unknown. Provincial militias were summoned into action only temporarily when pharaohs launched foreign adventures or needed troops for internal security and to protect frontiers or quarry expeditions. At first, the use of standing armies was mostly defensive. Troops were placed at fortifications protecting the Isthmus of Suez and the southern frontier on the Nile. The desert and the Mediterranean were natural defenses against possible enemies, but they didn't keep them out entirely. Battles erupted with Bedouins from eastern or western deserts and Nubians from Africa. When defeated, their soldiers became highly valued troops in the Egyptian army.

Finally, one man came out on top—Menthuhotep II. During his fifty-one-year reign, he reunified the country, placing the capital at Thebes, his power base in Upper Egypt, and giving Egypt a centralized government once again.

In this period of stability, called the Middle Kingdom, the rulers left pyramids of more modest size, though equally inspired by the need to provide entry to life in the hereafter. During this time, the royal administration was reformed and extended. The royal court required more scribes and more officials, which led to the expansion of a middle class who would serve their superiors faithfully. It was a prosperous time for Egypt. New towns were founded and stretches of desert were converted into farmland.

Egypt's rulers at the time believed their rightful place in the world was on top, dominating their neighbors. Theirs is a record of one conquest after another. They grabbed what they wanted, sometimes built fortresses with permanent garrisons, and expected annual tribute from their victims. Military campaigns to the south subjugated Nubia. Other expeditions were sent north into the Sinai Peninsula to mine for turquoise.

By Egyptian standards, the Middle Kingdom lasted only a short time—less than three hundred years—before a second collapse occurred. The era ended with the brief four-year reign of Sobeknefru, a female pharaoh. Only three more times in ancient Egypt's three thousand-year history would a woman become pharaoh. After Sobeknefru's reign came the Second Intermediate Period (1640–1550 B.C.), a time of foreign domination. Although the names of many kings of this period are known to us through archaeological finds, the rest is obscure. They were often non-royal persons who seized power. Asian in name, they were known by the Greek term, the Hyksos, which means "rulers of foreign countries." Sir Alan Gardiner, the Egyptologist, thinks they were Palestinians. Some, or most, were Semites, according to names on their seals. The Hyksos' physical appearance, says Guillemette Andreu, is shown in the tomb painting of a caravan of Palestinian traders. "The men have curly beards and frizzy hair; their loincloths are dyed and striped; and their feet are shod in lattice-work sandals. As for their women, they have light eyes and wear multicolored dresses and leather ankle boots."

The Hyksos never carried out a full-scale invasion of Egypt. Most likely, many arrived in Egypt as free persons, or as captives of foreign campaigns. Often they became completely Egyptianized (just as many immigrants to the United States become completely Americanized). While the Hyksos did not invade Egypt, they were able to take control of part of the country. Six of the Hyksos, once Palestinian local chiefs, became powerful enough to claim the throne of the pharaohs. They remained in the Nile Delta in the north at Avaris, unable to control the Egyptians in the south at Thebes. No royal Hyksos tomb has ever been discovered, nor any mummies. They seem to have tried to make peace with the Egyptians, adopting some of their ways, and their hieroglyphic writing as well.

The Hyksos brought significant changes in the civilization of Egypt. The most important was the introduction of the horse and the horse-drawn chariot, which would play a big part in Egypt's future. New types of daggers and swords, bronze weapons, the compound Asian bow, and a new kind of fortification were other benefits. From the Hyksos, the Egyptians also learned to improve their metalworking, weaving, and pottery techniques. In addition, they made alliances with some

BRONZE WEAPONS

The Hyksos introduced bronze weapons to the ancient Egyptians. Bronze is produced by using intense heat to combine copper with tin. It can be cast into any shape by using molds. That process led to a simpler way of making spearheads, arrowheads, and battle-axes. Bronze knife blades became longer and narrower and developed into a new weapon—the sword.

What the Bronze Age (roughly 2500–1000 B.C.) had introduced, the Iron Age—which began around 1000 B.C.—improved upon. Iron is even stronger and harder than bronze, and better suited to military needs. It is not scarce, and is widely distributed. Artisans learned to smelt iron ore and used it to produce weapons with a durable and lasting edge.

countries on the borders of Egypt. After a series of struggles with the last Hyksos rulers, the Egyptians at last forced their withdrawal. This marked the beginning of the New Kingdom, around 1550 B.C.

Before the Hyksos took power, the Egyptians considered themselves superior to all other peoples. The Hyksos conquest shattered that belief. After the Hyksos were forced out, Egypt's efforts to extend its empire in Asia made it impossible to ignore foreign ideas and practices. As trade expanded, more and more foreigners moved into Egypt, creating a richer mixture of people, ideas, and ways of living.

The historian Donald Spanel writes that "ironically, one of the greatest benefits of the Asians came with their withdrawal." As the Egyptian rulers pursued the Asians in the Near East, it brought them into greater contact with other peoples and cultures and led to more trading and military expeditions.

Back in power, the pharaohs sent armies into Palestine and Syria and established their rule as far as the Euphrates River. The troops in the new professional army came mostly from the fringes of the Egyptian world—Syria, Libya, and Nubia. These soldiers were mercenaries, paid from treasures taken from the defeated peoples and from taxes levied on them. The hired soldiers were stationed in garrison fortresses at strategic points throughout Egypt's empire, and kept in a high state of readiness for action.

What the army looked like can be gathered from bas-reliefs, paintings, and figures. On the march, the soldier wore a short loincloth and carried his shield and weapons in his hands. For hand-to-hand fighting, the weapons were the club, the ax, and the knife. To attack from a distance, they used bows and arrows, and sometimes the slingshot, which could hurl a missile or projectile a long way. To protect himself, the soldier had a large, rectangular shield made of wood covered with leather. It protected a man from his neck to his feet. A helmet and a coat of mail were added much later. The coat of mail was a leather jerkin covered with small metal scales— a Syrian invention.

These figures, found in the tomb of Prince Mesehti of the Eleventh Dynasty, are an example of what Egyptian soldiers may have looked like in ancient times.

The Egyptians borrowed the technique of chariot warfare from the Hyksos and made it their own. The chariot crew consisted of a driver, who carried a whip, and a fighting man, who used a bow and arrows and a dozen javelins. Infantry supported the charioteers.

Egyptian warfare included attacks on Palestine from time to time, to secure a buffer zone along the Isthmus of Suez. Other goals were to repel a raid by the "Sand-dwellers." Military campaigns in Nubia brought back red granite for the building of a king's pyramid. From Nubia came other products and materials Egyptians were fond of—gold, incense, ebony, oils and grains, leopard skins, elephant tusks "and every beautiful, valuable thing." Much of these items were given in tribute. A pharaoh might use other ways besides war to gain precious materials. For instance, the Egyptians established peaceful trading relations with Phoenicia so that they could import large loads of fir and cedar for boat-building and to make the coffins for nobles.

If the inscribed boasts of generals are to be believed, they were ruthless in victory—razing towns, cutting down fig trees and vineyards, and killing captives. When prisoners were taken alive, they were branded like cattle with the king's name, sorted into squads, and placed in the Egyptian army. From the New Kingdom on, when soldiers killed an enemy, they cut off one of his hands. These trophies were counted by the scribes, and then tossed in a pile before the king. That was how the king kept track of his "achievements."

Soldiering could be a profitable profession (if you survived). Besides the loot distributed after every victory, an especially courageous warrior was rewarded with a piece of land in his own town as well as slaves captured from the enemy. One soldier, for example, was granted nineteen slaves and several

Two Egyptian soldiers practice fighting to improve their combat skills.

gold necklaces and cups. After long and honorable service, another soldier is recorded as receiving an elegant two-story house, servants, a herd of cattle, and the promise of burial at the king's expense.

RAMESES II

Rameses II of the Nineteenth Dynasty led an army composed largely of mercenaries, against the Hittite stronghold—Kadesh. His army was made of 20,000 men, with 2,500 chariots. Though he held off the enemy, he was unable to capture Kadesh. Eventually he made peace, leaving the Hittites in control of most of Syria.

Rameses proved the quality of his leadership, but he was handicapped by outdated weapons. His enemies were equipped with new iron weapons, while Rameses' mercenaries were still using Bronze Age weapons. Rameses called the battle for Kadesh a triumph, proclaiming it on the walls of the buildings—some now say it is the first recorded battle in history. His texts on his victory were even used in schools as an exercise.

Army food usually included bread, beef, beer, cakes, vegetables, and other nourishing foods. Training took the form of route marches and single combat. The Egyptian kings liked to watch the fight and invited the court to enjoy it with them. When it came to the real thing, however, victory was as chancy as it has always been in warfare. The pride of the Egyptians made them reluctant to record their defeats, but enough evidence has been found to show that they did in fact lose battles sometimes, and badly.

Battles were governed by customs that seem strange to us today. An enemy might choose to conduct a purely defensive war, holding out from the shelter of his stronghold. But if he decided to meet the invader in the open, he was expected to propose a fixed time and place for the battle, and arrange it to suit the enemy's convenience as well. There were exceptions, though—the Hittites had no qualms about ambushing the Egyptians.

The Step Pyramid still stands today as a monument to King Djoser.

CHAPTER FIVE

BUILDING THE PYRAMIDS AND BEYOND

The Age of the Pyramids lasted for five centuries beginning with the Third Dynasty and ending with the Sixth Dynasty during the Old Kingdom. King Djoser, the first king of the Third Dynasty, built the Step Pyramid at Saqqara—the burial grounds in the city of Memphis on the west bank of the Nile. The pyramid is a massive structure rising in six unequal stages to a height of 204 feet (62 m). This earliest of pyramids forms the center of an excavated and restored complex of sacred buildings. Here the deceased king was meant to enjoy a beautiful and unending environment in which to live for eternity. The ancient Egyptian word for *pyramid* (which is Greek) is *mer*, meaning "place of ascension."

The renowned architect of the first pyramid was Imhotep. Later he displayed other talents as a writer and a physician. The early Egyptians credited Imhotep with the invention of building in stone—Djoser's monument was the first to be built entirely of that material. Earlier royal tombs had been made of brick, with only a small number made of granite and limestone. The Step Pyramid was not a flash of genius erected without preparation. It was the product of a cultural evolution going back to prehistoric Egypt. Those builders went through periods of apprenticeship with other materials, gradually acquiring the skills to create masterpieces. Their techniques improved from prehistoric shelters to huts made of reeds and palm ferns and coated with mud. These structures did not last, so the Egyptians continued to experiment with more permanent types of buildings. As the Egyptians searched for materials to support them in their eternal life, fortified mud-brick walls led to longer-lasting stone structures.

It was the permanence of stone that convinced Imhotep to use it for King Djoser's necropolis—a large, elaborate cemetery. The whole complex was built out of quarried stone over a maze of subterranean chambers that were built into the bedrock.

In time, the master builders realized that increasing the volume of the stone blocks would make the structure more stable, and allow them to build higher and higher. Imhotep kept changing plans till he reached the final form of a pyramid in durable, fine-quality dressed limestone. The white-stone pyramid totaled some 9 million cubic feet (254,852 cubic meters) of stonework.

The ancient Egyptians had easy access to good building stone along the desert escarpment that borders the Nile Valley. In a remarkably short time they had mastered the mason's skills. The mud-bricks used by earlier builders had to be small in size to allow uniform drying by the air. In building in stone, however, the vast labor of trimming stone to regular shapes makes it advantageous to build blocks as large as can be moved.

The pyramid form, according to Guillemette Andreu, a French Egyptologist, "symbolizes the ascent of the soul of the deceased to the powers of the sun and the sky. . . . The six steps of Djoser's pyramid evoke a gigantic staircase connecting his soul with the divine sun."

The Fourth Dynasty, which began about 2620 B.C., became known as the Golden Age of Pyramids. Until the rise of the New Kingdom (c. 1550 B.C.), all the pharaohs were buried in pyramids. Then, when the capital was moved to Thebes, the kings broke with the thousand-year-old tradition and chose the rock-cut tombs of the Valley of the Kings as their burial place.

Great master builders followed Djoser and Imhotep. They included Kings Snoferu, Khufu, and Khephren. Snoferu built the first true pyramid set on a square base. It had four great triangular faces converging to a point or apex. Unlike the step pyramid, it was planned from the start as a perfect three-dimensional pyramid shape. This one fell into ruins, but it was a great achievement. The same king had two other colossal pyramids built, not far from each another, both more than 310 feet (94 m) high.

After Snoferu, the pyramid builders moved north to Giza, almost opposite Cairo. King Khufu, the son of Snoferu, built the Great Pyramid at Giza in 2690 B.C. It rose to 481 feet (147 m). Its volume was 88 million cubic feet (2.5 million cubic meters). About thirty years later King Khephren built the second pyramid at Giza. These were known as the oldest among the Seven Wonders of the World, and they are the only ones to have survived intact. The pyramids that followed in the Fifth and Sixth Dynasties were more modest in size.

The pyramids of the pharaohs were not meant to stand alone. They were the heart of a great complex. The body of a king—brought to the burial site by boat—was taken into a temple built along a canal linked to the river by docks and piers. A paved and covered causeway extended to the foot of the pyramid. Inside, an upper sanctuary was provided for the ritual cult of the dead king. The complex also held a network of inner corridors, vaulted chambers, apartments, and storehouses. After the mortuary rites were completed, the mummified body was sealed inside the pyramid. Now the king was safe in his eternal residence.

King Khephren also built the Great Sphinx of Giza—a colossal creature crouching in the desert sand. It is 66 feet (20 m) high and 240 feet (73 m) long, combining the body of a lion and the head of the pharaoh, crouching in the desert sand. Its meaning has been considered for ages to be an unsolved mystery. Most scholars tend to think the king had it carved out of the knoll of rock close to his causeway, to suggest he had the power and grace of both man and lion. Whatever the truth, Khephren did not originate the model, and later it became a decorative motif throughout the world. To the Egyptians of his own time, the Sphinx was a god.

During the five centuries of the age of pyramids, the building and equipping of the funerary monuments was the largest industry in Egypt. When we look at these amazing structures, we cannot help but wonder who performed the labor, how such a mammoth project was organized, and what effect these marvels had on Egyptian civilization.

Behind the construction of the pyramids was the deep-rooted Egyptian belief that life would continue after death much as it was experienced on Earth. These rock tombs provided the home for the perishable body of the dead. To accomplish this on such a grand scale took great wealth, and the lengthy efforts of artisans and laborers who had to meet new demands in every reign of this period. The problem of designing and building the pyramids led to innovations in technology. Ancient cultures had no research laboratories whose aim was to invent or improve upon technology. Their creativity was exercised in trying to meet the practical necessities of design and construction.

The pharaohs in the age of the pyramids were tireless builders. They made sure that boundless energy and immense resources were devoted to the public works required by their worship of the gods. The responsibility was placed in the hands of the viziers who were called "overseers of all the works of the kings." And "all" meant not only the pyramids but also the irrigation projects, the canals, temples, and palaces.

Most important of these was the building of the royal pyramids. We know about the talented architects, such as Imhotep. But who did the backbreaking labor? The workforce was drawn from that vast mass of people—the peasants. These farmers were not enslaved, but during the time of year when their labor was not needed on the farms, they could be ordered to build major public projects such as the pyramids.

To the peasants, such forced labor was a great national necessity. They could not refuse. As the pharaoh's subjects, they were ready to obey his orders and to help shape Egypt as he wished. Some kings excused certain classes of people from

The peasants provided the labor for all sorts of projects from pyramids to temples to canals.

such labor, including the priests and the staff of the royal funerary complexes, and the scribes who served in government administration. At times, when peasants felt their labor was demanded too often, a spirit of revolt was kindled, and men would flee their homes rather than answer the vizier's call. If caught, deserters were sentenced to a beating, and if they repeated their desertion, they were assigned to other projects.

An important addition to the workforce in the New Kingdom came from prisoners of war—Asians and Nubians. Nubians were also used as police or soldiers. Some kings sent raiding forces into neighboring lands to bring back men they enslaved for labor of various kinds.

The work crews were organized in semi-military fashion—a basic unit of one hundred men, divided into groups of ten, with overseers. These crews would get the stone used to build tombs and other projects from mines and quarries. Most of these were in the eastern desert, between the Nile and the Red Sea, or in the Sinai Peninsula. Expert guides helped to locate new mines and quarries.

We know something of how the work was carried out because the laborers and the overseers carved graffiti on the rock walls, as well as inscriptions that tell us much about these expeditions. Workers had few tools. To shape the blocks, the stonecutters used a pick of hard, heavy basalt, held in their bare hands or fitted into wooden tongs, and also hardened copper chisels. If the rock was soft, they used a copper saw.

In one group of quarries, calcite—a stone that looks like alabaster—was found. It is hard to work, but good for carving statues, vases, and even small chapels. Its veins of marbled color were favored for delicate objects, especially jars or containers. From these same quarries a colossal statue was extracted, over 20-feet (6-m) high and weighing more than 70 tons. The stone was cut underground. The statue was sculpted in the open air and then attached to a sled with ropes holding it in place. The sled was hauled a distance of 9 miles (14 km) by a crew of 172 men. This feat was pictured in a tomb nearby, with image and text providing details.

Where to place a mighty pyramid? The pharaoh, with his vizier and architect, selected the site and decided on its size and orientation. The plateau of Giza, where the three Great Pyramids are located, was chosen for its visibility and its relative flatness, and because it was close to the high waters of the Nile's inundation. Only 1,000 yards (914 m) separated the construction site from the harbor where the stone was unloaded. Besides, close by Giza itself was a certain kind of stone needed for the pyramid's interior.

Archaeologists have not found any contemporary representation of how a pyramid was built. No vizier or architect left a depiction of or plan for a pyramid on the walls of his tomb. Nor has any diagram or text on papyrus been discovered for the pyramids, though some were found for the tombs in the Valley of the Kings. It took exhaustive research to figure out how these structures were developed into pyramids. Jean-Philippe Lauer, a French archaeologist, who began studying the site at Saqqara in 1926, was able to reconstruct the pyramid complex of King Djoser.

It is hard for us to imagine how the workers built such gigantic structures. Take the Khufu pyramid, 450 feet (137 m) high, and built about 4,500 years ago. It is composed of 2.3 million blocks of limestone, ranging from 2.5 to 15 tons, taken from quarries. The pyramid's total volume is 90 million cubic feet (2.5 million cu m). Its lower levels are made of stone blocks about 59 cubic feet (1.7 cu m) each. The blocks are smaller as the pyramid rises to its peak.

Some people believe that about 100,000 laborers built this pyramid, working in teams of some 20,000 men, rotated every few months. Think of the problems of housing, feeding, and caring for these workers, as well as the planning and management of their labor. That must have been an organizational achievement as great as the engineering of the project itself. The pyramid probably took about twenty years to build.

The workweek of the builders was nine days, with the tenth day set aside for leisure. On their free day, some men returned home to see their families. Remains of workers' huts have been found close by the site, designed to shelter twelve men, and containing kitchens and ovens for baking bread and brewing beer. Not long ago, in 1992, archaeologists found the tombs of some laborers who died on the job at Giza. Study of their skeletons showed all of them suffered serious spinal injury from the strain of hauling and carrying.

How were those huge blocks cut out of the quarries? The workers split off large pieces of limestone by inserting wedges of dry wood into small holes banged into the surface of the rock, along a sort of dotted line. They wet the wedges, and as the wood expanded, it broke off large pieces of rock. Then the workers cut these into smaller blocks.

The next challenge was to move these great chunks of stone to the site of the pyramid. Remember they did not have wheels at this time or domestic animals powerful enough to pull these loads, or cranes to lift them.

The first stage was to move the finished blocks toward the site by boats and barges. Reaching the piers of the valley temples along the Nile, the loads would then have to be transported overland to the place of construction.

The work was not done on wheels, but by sled. The supervisor harnessed teams of workers to sleds that they hauled over a route covered with layers of silt—always wetted down so that the sled's runners would slide along. Since the building site was high on the desert plateau, a series of ramps were built so that the load could be hauled upwards, stage by stage. And the same ramp system was used to move the blocks higher and higher up the pyramid itself.

Some historians claim that slaves were the labor force that built the pyramids. But many others, including Henri Stierlin, a specialist in architecture and ancient civilizations, argue that "slave labor would have affected the quality of the construction. Such perfection must have required an unshakable determination and patient teamwork, as well as absolute faith in the redeeming role of the pharaoh-god."

The historian Daniel Boorstin has pointed out that since the pyramids "overwhelm and dazzle us as great public works, might they not have impressed the people who built them?" Surely they were proud of their part in so great a work. Inscriptions on the stones they cut and moved tell of how "vigorous" or "enduring" a crew was. In our own time, when American workers built such immense projects as the Grand Coulee Dam or the Empire State Building, they too boasted of their role in these universally admired projects.

The pyramid laborers were paid in food from the king's granaries. Stierlin notes that this system, by giving the peasant crews more food than they raised for themselves, insured them against hunger in time of famine.

Later, in an era called the New Kingdom (1550 to 1070 B.C.), pharaohs built other types of structures. On the banks of the Euphrates River, the warrior-pharaoh Thutmose I erected a *stela* to proclaim this territory as Egypt's own. The stelae—large, round-topped stones that bear inscriptions and look like giant tombstones—often served the rulers of ancient Egypt as their official bulletin boards.

Egypt was now the wealthiest country in the Near East with tributes pouring in from all corners of the land. Thebes was the capital. A magnificent temple complex at Karnak dedicated to Amun-Re, the supreme state god, became the religious and political center of the empire.

Now, with the advent of the New Kingdom, Thutmose I had his secret tomb carved into the cliff of a desolate valley. His aim was to outwit tomb robbers. For generations to come, pharaohs followed his example. The area became known as the Valley of the Kings.

A portrait of King Tutankhamun that was found in his tomb.

KING TUT'S TOMB

For many of us, the most familiar pharaoh is Tutankhamun, or as he commonly is called King Tut. While his reign was brief—only nine or ten years—this young king became a household name when his tomb was discovered in 1922. It was the only largely undisturbed tomb of a pharaoh ever found. The fact that King Tutankhamun's tomb was fairly intact was of greater significance than the life of the man himself. The richness and variety of the treasures buried with the king made his tomb the most widely publicized archaeological discovery of the twentieth century. There are still studies to be done on Tutankhamun's treasures, now housed in the Egyptian Museum in Cairo.

The tomb was found in the Valley of the Kings at Thebes by British archaeologist Howard Carter and his wealthy backer, Lord Carnarvon. The tomb had apparently been entered by robbers at least twice, soon after the funeral. Substantial damage had been done, but the shrines and the sarcophagus—a coffin made of stone often decorated with writing—were untouched, probably because the robbers were caught in the act.

Inside the front room of the tomb were a superb throne, great couches and beds, chairs, painted and inlaid caskets, alabaster vases, chariots and boats, armchairs, plain chairs, stools, metal and stone vessels, every kind of weapon, walking sticks, ornaments, games, ritual objects, and more than a thousand pieces of valuable jewelry. Also found were a large number of dishes, with many kinds of food and drink the pharaoh would need in the afterlife.

After cataloging and removing everything from the front room, Carter and his expedition continued their exploration of the tomb. They discovered the burial chamber, and Carter went through several shrines before reaching the room that held the body of the young king.

Under the heavy stone lid of the sarcophagus, Carter discovered another coffin covered with a linen shroud. When that lid was rolled back, they saw a 7-foot (2-m) coffin bearing a likeness of Tutankhamun. Three other coffins were nested inside. When they got to the third, they saw that it was made of solid gold. A gold mask protected the head of the boy-king, but the rest of his body was in poor condition. A pitch-like substance on the mummy had attached it to the coffin. The excavators could not free it. An anatomist assigned to work with the body in the coffin unavoidably did much damage to it. Finally the work was completed. The experts estimated that Tutankhamun was nineteen at the time of his death.

During the New Kingdom, the most energetic builder to hold the throne of Egypt was Rameses II, king of the Nineteenth Dynasty. He dominated the thirteenth century B.C. and left behind more memorials than any other pharaoh. He succeeded to the throne at the age of twenty-five, and reigned for sixty-six years, outliving several of his children. And they were many, for Rameses had at least two principal wives, and many lesser ones. He also had a harem that included Hittite, Syrian, and Babylonian princesses. In his later years, he boasted of having fathered more than one hundred sons and daughters.

Rameses could never have enough of commemorating his fame. He took over many older statues or buildings, hacked off earlier inscriptions, and substituted his own, carving his name so deep that no one in the future could erase it. But he also built new works on an immense scale. His rock temple at Abu Simbel in Nubia holds four 67-foot (20-m) colossal seated statues of himself, facing the river. It was built to serve the ruler's cult. This famous structure faced destruction in modern times when Egypt wanted to cover it with water as part of its Aswan High Dam project. The United Nations Educational, Scientific and Cultural Organization (UNESCO) successfully campaigned to save it in the 1960s.

Rameses also built a large mortuary temple, called the Ramesseum, on the west bank of the Nile at Thebes. Although it was the largest tomb in the Valley of the Kings, little of it remains. Rameses added to the temples at Karnak and Luxor, and created a new city, Piramesse, in the Nile Delta region.

To build these grand monuments, the pharaoh relied on the

work of anonymous laborers that enabled him to claim the proud title of "Rameses the Great." The laborers' main job was to mold and stack unbaked brick for many uses. Government buildings and private homes too were made mostly of brick. When Rameses decided to build his new city, he rounded up the Israelites living in Egypt and forced them to mold bricks. Such work was usually done by foreigners, with prisoners of war or free men forced to labor.

The work was monotonous, but not difficult. Nile mud was mixed with chopped straw, moistened, trodden out for a time, and stirred now and then. The brick-maker filled his mold with the damp compound, and lifted it off, leaving the brick intact. After drying for eight days, the brick was ready for use. The work was usually done near a pool so that water-carriers could bring water to the brick-makers. Other workers gathered the stubble from harvested fields so that the chopped straw could be prepared.

Workers, according to ethical custom, were not supposed to be forced to work unreasonably hard. However, during the late New Kingdom, workers in one village complained of delays in getting their allotments of food and clothing so that their families went hungry. In one recorded instance they threatened to quit, moved menacingly to raid the supply warehouse, but stopped short of breaking in. One of their leaders spoke up: "We have come because we are desperate with hunger and thirst. We have no cloth, no oil, no fish, no vegetables. Send to our lord Pharaoh, send to our lord the king that he may give us the necessities of life." The workers appealed to a magistrate, who ordered a scribe to see that the protesters were given their food ration each day.

The threatened strike was called off. Working conditions were tolerable when masters took pains to provide decent housing, food, and clothing at regular intervals, and even to offer something extra now and then. Holidays and feast days came often, which helped morale. There was the chance too that highly skilled and responsible workmen might become foremen or overseers. But in troubled times the labor force was always the first to feel the stress and to suffer the most.

For the monuments Rameses II and other pharaohs built, the limestone and quartzite came from quarries on either side of the Nile Valley. Rameses kept the quarries in full operation. One day, while he was present, a single block larger than a granite obelisk was cut. Rameses knew instantly what to do with it. As he watched them day after day, his artisans shaped it into the form of a colossal statue—named Rameses-the-God.

When a pharaoh planned a huge enterprise it required the mobilization of a veritable army of specialists and laborers. For one such project, a pharaoh called up 9,368 men, including priests, engineers, scribes, police, cooks and bakers, artists, sculptors, master quarrymen, stone dressers, draftsmen—and these were only a small part of the team. The majority of workers hauled the stone on sleds or carried the necessary provisions.

Lacking the modern tools and equipment we now take for granted, the quarrying work was extremely primitive. It began with any boulders near at hand, big enough to use as a sarcophagus, a statue, or a group of figures. First, stone blocks nearest the road were removed. Then workers had to climb up the slope and roll great huge stones to the bottom, but this often shattered them. One day an overseer said, why don't we build a sloping road beside this hill, and let the blocks slide down it? His idea worked beautifully. Ten blocks—each about some 7 feet (2 m) in length—suitable for great statues, were brought down unharmed. It was a brilliant achievement. "It had taken a mere thousand years to discover," commented an Egyptologist.

Many of the quarrymen and stone workers were either prisoners-of-war or convicted criminals. Not all—because some free Egyptians chose this kind of work. Did they love to labor in the quarries? Apparently not. At the end of the Rammesid Dynasty, the power of the pharaohs weakened and civil wars broke out as the Third Intermediate Period began. The quarry workers quit their jobs and roved the countryside, "committing countless deeds of sacrilege and brutality," says Professor Montet, "which hardly suggests that they had previously been content with their lot."

An artisan chisels a golden bowl in this wall painting in the tomb of Rekhmere, a vizier, in the Eighteenth Dynasty.

CHAPTER SIX

THE BEAUTY OF CRAFT WORK

In building the pyramids, common laborers were the foundation upon which the great superstructures rested. For items of everyday life, however, ancient Egyptians relied on the skills of another group—the artisans or craftspeople. Among the oldest skills were those of the stonemason, the shipbuilder, the wood worker, the potter, the goldsmith, and the weaver.

What we know about their crafts comes to us mostly through the depictions and the objects of everyday life gathered in the tombs. We don't know whether the artisans were organized into guilds, as they would be in medieval times. The level of skill reached by the metal and woodworkers match the best in the modern world. Goldsmiths were valued so highly that they were made members of the royal court. And their achievement in carpentry is clear from examination of the chests, chairs, boats, and coffins found in Tutankhamun's tomb, as well as others.

Carpenters had a hard time obtaining the best woods for their work. Local wood was rare and poor in quality, but they had to make do with it for the more routine jobs. The pharaohs and the nobles demanded better, however, and sent expeditions into the heart of Africa for ebony and to Lebanon for cedar. Their tools were axes, saws, drills, chisels, adzes, awls, and the ruler—still in use everywhere. Scrawled on walls we see friendly warnings: "Take another saw, this one is hot!" or "Watch out for your fingers!"

Potters had much less trouble getting their raw material. They only had to go to the desert, or lean over the banks of the Nile to gather clay for ceramics. Then they stamped on the clay, kneaded it, and mixed it with water to produce the smooth paste they shaped on the wheel.

Potters supplied pots, plates, cups, tumblers, vases, and jars that every household needed. The earthenware was fired in kilns and finished cold. Ceramicists then treated the outer surface to give it a polished look, and they might decorate pieces with designs in black or white paint, or in red or blue.

A potter's life was neither easy nor valued. Their work was looked down on as simply utilitarian, manual labor. Nor were tanners and cobblers rated any better. Leatherwork in Egypt

This wall painting shows potters making vases during the Eighteenth Dynasty.

was done as far back as prehistoric times. Workshops produced a variety of goods, from royal manuscript cases to helmets, quivers, bucklers (small, round shields), and sandals. Tanners and cobblers knew how to emboss leather, often with delicate ornamental themes, but they never used any tanning process except oiling.

AN ANCIENT SCULPTOR SPEAKS

Little is known about how artisans viewed their own work. Here and there, scraps of evidence have been found, such as this one, testifying to what a sculptor thinks of his own skill:

I am an artist that excels in my art, a man above the common herd in knowledge. I know the proper attitude for a statue [of a man], I know how a woman holds herself . . . the way a man poises himself to strike with the harpoon, the look in an eye at its moment, the bewildered state of a man roused from sleep, the way a spearman lifts his arm, the tilt of a runner's body. I know the secret of making inlays that fire cannot melt or water dissolve. There is no man famous for this knowledge other than I myself and my own eldest son . . .

Women had one craft all to themselves. That is, until technological changes made the craft more attractive to men. Spinning and weaving was carried on in women's workshops. Looms were horizontal, and placed on the ground until the end of the Middle Kingdom. That meant women had to work bent over, or sitting on the floor. When the easier vertical loom came into use in the New Kingdom, men gradually replaced women in the workshops.

As chariots were introduced early in the New Kingdom, a new trade was created. It was really a specialized branch of carpentry, for the vehicles were basically constructed of wood. A great many parts went into a chariot—fifty or more. Even the wheels were made of wood; metal was never used. The circle of the wheel was made by joining several segments cut from wood of the proper thickness.

Ancient Egyptians made offerings to Hathor, goddess of the sky, love, beauty, and fertility.

CHAPTER SEVEN

GODS AND BELIEFS

When Herodotus, the early Greek historian, visited Egypt in the fifth century B.C., he was struck by how intensely religious the Egyptians were. They looked upon the gods as owners of the whole universe. Anything good that befell Egypt was credited to the gods. If a pharaoh won a victory in battle or escaped a trap laid by an enemy, it happened because his appeal for help had reached the gods' ears. If fine weather interrupted a bad season during a royal wedding ceremony, it was attributed to divine favor. So too when well diggers found water in the desert.

As for ordinary people, their modest wishes were also respected by the gods. Everyone believed that the gods pitied the poor. Even when a run of bad luck upset a man, he was sure that the gods would one day sustain him.

The number and diversity of Egyptian divinities astonished foreign observers. Papyruses depict the crocodile and the bull as widely worshipped gods. The ibis and the falcon were regarded as sacred birds all over Egypt. A cat was the center of cat worship. And plants as well as animals were venerated by the pious. Every town, big or small, had its sacred tree, just as it had its local deity. The sycamore is depicted with men and women approaching it with outstretched hands to receive the holy water sprinkled by a goddess hidden inside the tree.

The temple was the focal point of Egyptian life. It was the house of a god where he or she was worshiped as the source of all blessings. But it was also the center of economic and intellectual activity. Every temple was like a miniature town. A great number of religious structures have survived in the Nile Valley. These structures are signs of a culture permeated by religious values. Religious structures were built of durable stone rather than the unbaked brick used for secular structures. Each god in the seemingly infinite pantheon had his or her own temple or altar.

Each temple was of a standard type, regardless of its size. All temples contained the same elements. Each was built in a large area surrounded by a wall of large, unbaked bricks. The wall usually enclosed less important religious buildings— service facilities, warehouses, and the homes of priests and administrative staff. The sanctuary inside the temple contained the shrine holding the image of the god to whom the temple was dedicated.

Entry to the priesthood came through nomination by the king or his delegate. Such appointments, religious or not, were hereditary. However, the king could override the family succession and name the priest himself whenever he wished.

When an Egyptian priest entered the service of a god, he became part of a rigid hierarchy. At the top was the high priest. Each temple, large or small, was set up as an entirely independent and self-governing organization. The priests were at the service of a god who was worshiped in one place and in one temple. Each town had its own gods, unconnected to those of neighboring towns. Throughout Egypt's long history, it seems clear that the gods were local deities. With all the deities keeping their independence, a polytheistic

This sculpture shows a priest of the temple of Thoth, the god of learning and wisdom.

system of religion—the worshiping of more than one god—developed. There appears to have been a very high number of parallel religions.

In a sense, that fragmentation was overcome by the figure of the pharaoh. When the country was unified by the military conquest of the north by the south, the pharaoh emerged as a god-like figure. His task was to govern Egypt. He was destined to return to heaven after death. It was up to him to ensure peace between the order that regulated the life of the universe and that part of the created world—Egypt—that he had been entrusted to govern. So he belonged to both the world of the humans and the world of the gods. His was the religious and secular task of preserving relationships with the gods and making sure that Egypt would be protected by them. In this sense, he was the high priest to all the gods. The high priests of each temple were thus stand-ins for the pharaoh.

The temple was the house of the deity, not the worshipers, who were normally forbidden to see the god's statue. The god was visible to the worshipers only during the occasion of festivals or processions held to show the god to the faithful.

The priesthood consisted mostly of men, with women assigned to specialized roles—and having less power than the men. Priests made offerings on the altar, recited prayers, took care of the statue, treating it as though it were human through precise rituals, in ceremonies that took up most of the day. They also arranged for the statue's periodic trips outside the temple. On those occasions, the faithful had the chance not only to see the god but to ask him questions about their problems, large or small, with the priests acting as intermediaries. Priests also acquired fame as sages and scholars. They created the Houses of Life annexed to the temples, which functioned as cultural and educational as well as religious institutions. In this way, they passed on Egypt's cultural heritage to the young.

Not all pharaohs saw the value of the priesthood. One of the pharaohs, Amenhotep IV (1353–1336 B.C.), broke with the priesthood, and tried to shift the religion of Egypt from polytheism to a kind of monotheism—to transform the nation from one that believed in many gods to one that had only one god. He wanted the people to worship solely the sun god Aton. Although he reigned less than twenty years, he created a much disputed period in history. He exploited his absolute power to become a royal revolutionary.

Amenhotep IV changed his name to Akhenaton (servant of Aton), and took on the role of high priest, celebrating the new god. He tried to suppress all rival gods, and to make the worship of Aton—and himself as son of Aton—the only religion of the empire. He closed the old temples, and obliterated the name of Amon, the Egyptian god of life, from many public inscriptions. He held that life after death could not be realized unless by the gift of the pharaoh. In the end, he provoked resistance from believers in the traditional religion.

Akhenaton, with perhaps a few thousand of his devoted followers, moved the capital from Thebes to a remote desert

Akhenaton forced his people to worship only one god—Aton.

site at Amarna in Middle Egypt. His workers built a new city, with a huge royal palace, perhaps the largest in the ancient world at that time.

The new capital was designed to fit the new religion. Worship of the sun god could not take place in the secret recesses of closed temples, as the priests were accustomed to do before Akhenaton took power. Only an open courtyard where the rays of the sun could be felt directly was acceptable to Aton. So Akhenaton's architects planned his new capital city to that end.

Sculpture and painting too were influenced in the direction of a freer and more natural style. According to their beliefs, nature and humankind must be depicted as they are. The artists tried to capture human emotion and the feeling of time passing, breaking with the tradition of monumentality and timelessness.

The new religion lasted as long as Akhenaton ruled. Upon his death, however, his religious movement collapsed. And the priests and nobles whose privileges he had attacked did all they could to wipe out every trace of his reign. From this time on, though the pharaohs were still officially gods, the priests kept close watch on them. No major enterprise could be launched without consulting the oracle of Amun. And since the priests interpreted the oracle, theirs was the ultimate voice.

This photograph shows the mummy of a priestess.

CHAPTER EIGHT

MAKING MUMMIES

Egypt is often thought of as "the land of the mummies." But where does the term *mummy* come from? It applies to the body of a human, animal, bird, fish, or reptile that has been preserved by artificial means. The word *mummia* meant "preserved bodies" in the Middle Ages. Persians visiting Egypt saw some embalmed corpses and mistook the darkened resin that coated those bodies to be *mummia*, their word for *bitumen*, the substance made from tar, asphalt, or crude petroleum. Finally the word *mummy* came to be used for the body underneath that coating.

When did people get the idea of preserving the body for an

indefinite time? It was probably before the first dynasties, when Egyptians saw how unchanged the bodies of the dead were after years of burial. Because of the extreme dryness of the climate and soil in Egypt, the bodies of the dead became mummified naturally. Noting this, the Egyptians developed techniques that improved on the natural effects of desert burial. To reunite the spiritual and physical elements of persons after death, it was necessary to preserve the integrity of the body and prevent its decay. The chief aim of every Egyptian was to preserve the body in order to attain everlasting life. To that cult of the dead, with its preservation of the mummy, we owe much of what we know about ancient Egypt.

Once an Egyptian had fitted out his tomb—his "house of eternity"—he was ready to "cross to the other bank." The Egyptians referred to death in this way because they disliked the word *die*. Upon a person's death, the body was handed over to professional embalmers. Mummification took place in workshops attached to the various necropolises. The embalmers supplied most of the funerary equipment. Mummification methods varied by time and location, but especially with the wealth and status of the dead. Egyptian embalmers might be honest or not, conscientious or careless, as X rays of mummies have shown.

A mummification of the best quality required much time and care. The brain was extracted through the nose by a hook, or by an incision in the skull. The brain was then discarded because the Egyptians believed humans thought with their heart, not their brain. All the internal organs but the heart were removed. These organs were tied up in separate packages and placed in four

Canopic jars, such as these, were used to store the internal organs of the deceased.

alabaster vases called canopic jars that would be enclosed in the tomb so that the deceased would have them in the next world.

The body cavity was cleaned out twice, and filled up with aromatic spices. Next, it was immersed in natron (anhydrous sodium carbonate), a naturally occurring substance used for many purposes, including house-cleaning. After seventy days, the body was again washed and then wrapped in rolls of linen soaked in gum. Many different substances were needed for the complete procedure. According to the archaeologist Pierre Montet, they included "beeswax to cover ears, eyes, nose, mouth and the incision made by the embalmers, cassia, cinnamon, cedar oil (actually derived from the juniper tree), gum, henna, juniper berries, onions, palm wine, various types of resin, sawdust, pitch, tar, and of course, the indispensable natron."

But there was more to be done. The mummy must now be dressed, and adorned with necklaces, amulets, bracelets, and rings. Often a copy of the *Book of the Dead*—a collection of about two hundred spells, incantations, prayers, and hymns—to ensure resurrection in the next world, was placed between the legs. The body and limbs were wrapped in linen, and a mask placed over the face. For kings and nobles, the mask was made of gold. The mummy was then wrapped in a shroud.

Now the mummy was placed in a case of wood, shaped like a human figure, and the image of the person was painted on the top. The coffin of a pharaoh or a noble was then placed inside a huge stone sarcophagus. Within the coffins and on the walls of the tombs, magic texts were written or painted to help the person in the afterlife.

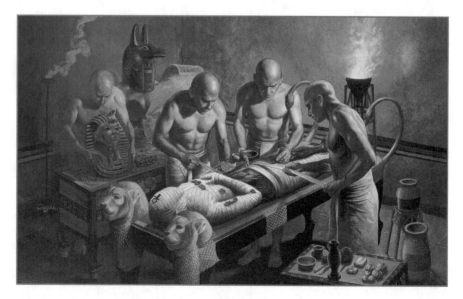

Workers prepare the deceased's body for burial.

On the funeral procession to the site of the burial, mourners included family, friends, and servants. Their grief was voiced long and loud. Those who could afford it hired at least two professional mourners to grieve openly while the dead person was being mummified, and to follow the funeral cortege, or procession, to the tomb. Many women made a career of mourning. These mourners represented the goddesses Isis and Nephthys—the sisters and mourners of Osiris, a god associated with the dead and the underworld. After the procession came the descent into the tomb. The sarcophagus was placed on its square stone receptacle, and near it the chest with the alabaster jars and the things that would be most useful in the hereafter, including food.

At the end of the seventy-day period, and just before burial, a ceremony called the "Opening of the Mouth" was carried out, so that the body would be able to perform "normal" functions in the hereafter—breathing, moving around, and eating the offerings buried in the tomb.

Afterwards, when everyone had withdrawn, a mason walled up the doorway to the tomb. The company of mourners would gather nearby to eat and drink and listen to the music of harpists. The mourners would then go back to town, far more cheerful than when they left.

Such was the funeral of a wealthy Egyptian. Less well-off people were treated far more simply. The body was not opened and the internal organs were not removed. Instead, the body was pickled by natron injected through the rectum. The mummy was then put in a coffin and taken to an old unused tomb that had been turned into a communal burial place. The tomb was stacked to the roof with coffins. The mummy was equipped modestly for the next world—maybe with some tools, a pair of sandals, a bracelet, an amulet, or miniature figures of gods. The very poor—like today's homeless—even got shorter shrift. Their mummies, wrapped in coarse cloth or in rush mats were placed in a burial pit, and covered with a layer of sand.

Royal tombs were vulnerable to theft during periods when the authority of the pharaohs weakened. In the Third Intermediate Period, around 1075 B.C., robbers broke into tombs in the Valley of the Kings and plundered them. They showed no respect for the mummies, tearing them apart in their greed for gold and jewelry.

When some of the thieves were caught and put on trial, their testimony was recorded on papyrus. In this passage, a tomb robber confesses to what he did:

The noble mummy of this king was all covered with gold, and his inner coffins were bedizened with gold and silver inside and outside with inlays of all kinds of precious stones. We appropriated the gold which we found on this noble mummy of this god and on his eye amulets and his ornaments which were at his neck and on the inner coffins in which he lay. [We] found the royal wife just likewise and we appropriated all that we found on her too. We set fire to their inner coffins. We stole their outfit which we found with them, consisting of objects of gold, silver, and bronze, and divided them up among ourselves. We made this gold which we found on these two gods and on their mummies, their eye amulets and ornaments and their inner coffins into eight [parts].

These successful raids on tombs often occurred in times of economic stress. The robbers were usually the men who had built the tombs. They knew where every corridor in the maze led, and which rooms held the treasure. Besides the tomb workers, some corrupt officials also helped themselves to buried riches.

Fearing robbery, one pharaoh of the Old Kingdom had his pyramid designed so that the entrance leading to the burial chamber would not be in the usual position, in the north side of the superstructure. Instead, his architect placed the entrance outside the pyramid itself. Even so, somehow thieves got in and ruthlessly plundered the burial chamber.

Almost from the time the powerful kings of the Eighteenth to Twentieth Dynasties (1550-1150 B.C.) reigned from Thebes, their tombs were violated and plundered by the people of that capital. When all the gold and other precious items were gone, only the coffins and corpses remained to be salvaged. Still, the mummies of nine kings and many of their queens were found later, as well as the intact coffins of high priests and their female companions. Their mummies and the inscriptions in the tombs proved to be of great value to the archaeologists. The last royal mummies to be discovered were the three pharaohs found by Pierre Montet at Tanis in the Nile Delta in the 1930s. Not a single pharaoh has been found since, though many are still missing.

What may enormously enrich our understanding of life in ancient Egypt is the recent excavation of a necropolis, which may contain as many as ten thousand graves. The site is a 2-mile (3-km) square out in the Bahriya Oasis. For quantity and quality,

PALEOPATHOLOGY: A NEW SCIENCE

Mummies have a lot to teach us about disease too. A relatively new science called paleopathology is using modern research tools to learn about diseases in ancient times. The aim is to understand how diseases begin, spread, and die out. By analyzing Egyptian mummies and comparing the frequency of their pathological conditions with those of people today, we may find out whether our way of life causes specific diseases.

The earliest work in this field was done by French medical scientist Armand Ruffer. In 1909 he published his studies of many fragments of mummies from about 1085 B.C. He found that some medical problems of ancient Egypt were remarkably like those of modern Egyptians.

The many research specialists who have followed Ruffer have gradually improved on this work by using such techniques as the X ray, the microtome, the electron microscope, radiocarbon dating, and the CAT scan. Researchers have also found it possible to clone DNA taken from four-thousand-year-old bodies.

The discoveries made thus far include the finding that ancient Egyptians suffered from bilharzia, a worm infestation that also affects modern Egyptians. Another discovery is that ancient Egyptians had a great degree of dental wear and tear because the desert sand infiltrated their food, and literally ground down their teeth. Inhaling desert sand and cooking over fires also caused pneumoconiosis, a lung disease.

Generally, one can conclude that there were almost certainly class and gender differences in the health conditions of the ancient Egyptians. Women had a shorter life expectation, mostly due to the complications of childbearing. On the whole, upper-class people were most likely in better shape than peasants and slaves. People in such risky professions as metalworking may well have suffered from lung cancer. Epidemic diseases also had some effect. On at least one occasion, Egyptian soldiers brought back some kind of plague from their wars against the Hittites. Modern discoveries suggest that tuberculosis and polio were also problems.

said one of the archaeologists, "This is the most important discovery." The lavish mummies found in vaults carved into rock show they were wealthy dignitaries. As the study continues, it is expected that countless details of Egypt's Greco-Roman era will come to light.

From the Rhind papyrus, researchers have learned that ancient Egyptians were able to solve complex mathematical problems.

CHAPTER NINE

CALENDARS, CLOCKS, AND CURES

When you think of science, you may imagine a scientist working over a microscope or conducting experiments in a lab somewhere. The ancient Egyptians lacked our modern technology, but they performed some of the very earliest forms of scientific research. "From the Old Kingdom on," says Guillemette Andreu, an Egyptologist, "scholars conducted experiments and made fundamental discoveries which they recorded in treatises that would be improved over the centuries but always consulted. Scholars and priests tirelessly drew up lists of significant objects or events from nature or society."

The ancient Egyptians believed that the world was created by the gods and was knowable to humans. They compared data and analyzed what they observed to develop step-by-step procedures. The three realms of knowledge they especially sought to enlarge were mathematics, astronomy, and medicine. The decimal system we use goes back to an important series of

The wall carving shows ancient Egyptian symbols for numbers. The upside down "U" stands for ten.

discoveries made by Egyptian scholars starting about 3000 B.C. It started with the ten fingers we have, which we use to count. Hieroglyphic signs were invented to denote units of tens, hundreds, and thousands. The ways of doing arithmetic were spread by the schools.

The Egyptians also devised the first and most precise calendar that was known for millennia. Their year consisted of 12 months, each of 30 days, with 5 additional days at the end of the year, making 365 in all. Scholars believe their calendar originated for purely practical reasons. With the rising of the Nile, the main event in Egyptian life, people were always observing and averaging the time intervals between the arrival of the Nile floods.

They saw the year as a cycle of three seasons of the same duration—the four months when the Nile overflowed its banks (Akhet), the four of the cool season when the seed was sown (Peret), and the four of the time of harvest and heat (Shemu).

They linked the beginning of the new year to the rising of the Dog Star, Sirius—the brightest star in the heavens. Once a year, Sirius rose in the morning in direct line with the rising sun. That was a very important time for the Egyptians, the day the flooding of the Nile began. The only weakness of the Egyptian astronomers was failing to take leap years into account.

The Egyptians numbered the years according to a particular pharaoh's reign rather than in linear succession. Thus, to specify a date, they wrote: "Year 2 of the reign of [name of king], 4th month of Shemu, Day 12." The Egyptians divided day and night into 12 hours each. But they do not seem to have subdivided the hour into minutes and the minutes into seconds.

Standing on the rooftops of their temples, priests observed the sky and its constellations. They noted that stars were grouped around planets, which they called "the unwearying stars." They named five of the planets—Mars, Saturn, Jupiter, Venus, and Mercury—using Egyptian names.

The invention of the sundial or shadow clock was another Egyptian contribution to the science of time. Their shadow clock was a horizontal bar about 1 foot (30 centimeters) long, with a small T-shaped structure at one end. The T cast a shadow along the bar that was marked to measure the passage of time. The bar was set with the T facing east in the morning. Around noon it was reversed so that the T faced west until sundown.

But getting the precise time on the sundial was a shaky business. Suppose the sun went behind a cloud? And what about when it went down at night? So only the brightest hours were measurable, and even those times were rough estimates.

The next step toward accuracy was to create a timepiece that could measure both day and night without regard to weather or sun. That innovation was the water clock. About five hundred years after the first sundials, inventors began measuring the passage of time by the amount of water that dripped from a pot. Imaginative people came up with many forms of the clock. But all the forms did the same thing—they measured the amount of water passing through a hole. The

Egyptians made an alabaster vessel with a scale marked inside and a single hole at the bottom. They watched the water drip out of the hole, and measured the passage of time by the fall in the water level from one mark to the next. The water clock had no competition for thousands of years. It was the most accurate device for measuring time when the sun was not shining.

Along with developing new ways to measure time, the ancient Egyptians worked on ways to treat and cure illnesses. In ancient Egypt, medicine was known as "the necessary art." It was a carefully regulated profession, with many specialist branches. The goddess of medicine was Sekhmet, and the priests who trained in her temples were reputed to be the best physicians. Lay doctors were doctors who practiced clinical medicine together with magic in treating their patients. A third kind of physician had no medical training. He used only incantations, amulets, and magic to cure his patients. In theory, treatment was free, but the ability to make gifts to the doctor must have had an influence on a person's access to treatment and the quality of care.

The greatest need for medical care was in the villages. One historian calls the villages "loathsome pools of infestation." Many endemic diseases hit the well-off classes too, but the peasants suffered far more. Weakened by hard labor and bad nutrition, they were easy prey to disease. Several diseases were common in the villages—the eye disease ophthalmia, the infectious fluke disease, schistosomiasis, hepatitis, a Guinea worm disease, and amoebic dysentery, which since antiquity through today has never ceased to afflict both the rural and urban population of Egypt. These are parasitic diseases, caused by water-borne organisms. They are transmitted to humans through drinking water or by penetrating mucous membranes.

In the documents we meet not only general practitioners, but also surgeons, ophthalmologists, dentists, and other specialists. They range in rank from the beginning intern to the chief physician, who might be attached to the king, the court, or the nobility. The medical texts show that recourse to magic was a last resort, used only when standard medical or surgical procedures were not successful.

In one papyrus—65 feet (20 m) long and written about 1500 B.C.—seven hundred medical prescriptions are listed, classified by illnesses and the body organs involved. Another papyrus, a surgical treatise, is a 16-foot (5-m) roll about 3,600 years old. It deals with the care of wounds and fractures and describes forty-eight surgical operations. Still another papyrus is considered the first textbook of gynecology in medical history.

Research on skeletons and mummies carried on by paleopathologists working at archaeological sites also supplies much information. These scientists have concluded that tuberculosis, smallpox, tetanus, polio, and many parasitic diseases were common in ancient Egypt.

What about the treatments? Remedies listed in the text cover a rich variety: potions, pills, dressings, ointments, poultices, eyedrops, and enemas. Some of these treatments were effective while others failed or even caused some damage.

A pharaoh makes an offering to Isis, the mother goddess of fertility and nature.

This photograph shows the remains of a temple devoted to Horus and Sobek.

This carving depicts priests who worshiped Aton, the sun god. The carving was found in Amarna, Egypt, and dates back to 1340 B.C.

A priest stands behind women in mourning. It was important to the ancient Egyptians to show their grief, and sometimes they even hired women to act as mourners.

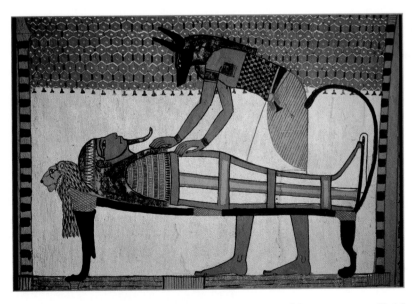

Anubis, the god of the dead, leans over the mummy of Sennutem, an official from the Eighteenth Dynasty.

Ancient Egypt had many different types of medical practitioners. This wooden panel shows a high official who was the chief of dentists and physicians.

This item was used to hold different medical ointments for the sick.

Many believed that the priests that studied medicine in the temples of Sekhmet, the goddess of medicine, were the doctors in ancient Egypt.

King Tutankhamun's wife anoints her husband with oil.

This wall painting shows Nefertiti, the main wife of Amenhotep IV, playing a game of senet, which is often compared to chess.

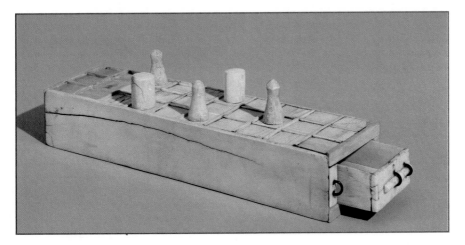

To win a game of senet, a player needed to get all seven of his or her pieces off the board.

Musicians often performed to entertain guests at banquets or other special events.

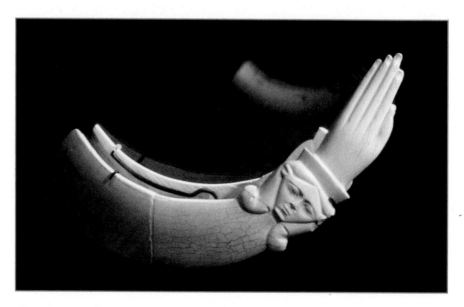

Clappers, one of the many musical instruments used by the Egyptians, were played by striking the pieces, or "hands," together.

Workers prepare medical treatments in a temple.

Many of these medicines were compounds of herbs found among the country's plants. Much of our knowledge of drugs and plants useful in medicine was first established by the Egyptians. Credit them with the introduction of castor oil as an effective remedy. It's estimated that at least one-third of the medicinal plants we use today were known to the ancient Egyptians.

This palette from the Early Dynastic Period shows pictures of animals and trees, which may have been used to keep records of livestock or crops.

CHAPTER TEN

THE INVENTION OF HIEROGLYPHICS

Scholars believe writing developed in the Middle East around 4000 B.C. As those Middle Eastern societies became more and more complex, with laws and edicts and rules of commerce, and thus the need for administrative record-keeping, some means of communication other than speech became necessary.

Speech came long before the written word, of course. Speech enabled us to exchange ideas, wishes, and questions with our fellow humans. Writing built on the same foundation, substituting visual for audible signs.

Some people think that writing was invented for commercial

reasons. Suppose you wanted to remember that a certain number of cattle belong to this family, not that? Or suppose you wanted to let someone know that a certain number of cattle were being transported to a particular place? A written sign served as a memory aid: a picture of the animal represented the animal, so that someone reading the sign knew the deal was in cattle, how many cattle, and perhaps the names of the buyer and the seller.

This was a kind of memory and, at the same time, the record of a transaction—a document created by a scribe. The document was inscribed on tablets of clay. The inventor of the first written document must have seen that it was much easier to have permanent records on tablets than try to hold all the information in his or her head. For one thing, people could store an endless amount of information on tablets, far more than they could hold in memory. Also, information could be retrieved at any time, without having to rely on one person's memory. So whatever people needed—an order, an account, a number, a name, or an idea—they could get hold of without having to find the message-giver. Almost magically, something imagined or noted could be passed on through space and time.

"Since the earliest vestiges of prehistoric civilization," says the historian Alberto Manguel, "human society has tried to overcome the obstacles of geography, the finality of death, the erosion of oblivion. With a single act—the incision of a figure on a clay tablet—that first anonymous writer suddenly succeeded in all these seemingly impossible feats."

That first writer conceived a new art of making marks in a piece of clay. But his writing would be meaningless unless another art was created—reading. The writer set down a message. The reader recognized its meaning.

Writing probably developed in Mesopotamia, and soon after in Egypt as well. Literacy—the ability to read and write—offered great new possibilities. Records made by scribes could be kept and consulted. Now it was easier to plan and keep track of the complex work of irrigation, land cultivation, harvesting, and taxing that a growing society needed. It strengthened government and its administration immensely. However, no more than 3 to 5 percent of the people in ancient times could read or write.

The earliest Egyptian writing that came to light consisted of a series of pictures of animate and inanimate objects. These inscriptions at very early sites in Upper Egypt indicate that writing went back a very long way—to the time of the formation of the Egyptian state shortly before 3000 B.C.

The signs used were pictures whose shapes designated real things, such as animals, plants, weapons, buildings, tools, furniture, people, and gods. If a person wanted to write about a pig or a baby, he or she could draw a pig or a baby. But how could people express abstract ideas, such as "to love," or "to be sad," or "to think"? Someone figured out that the same signs could be used, not for what they pictured, but for their phonetic values. For example, "bee" plus "leaf" equals belief. For a true writing system to work, there must be agreement that sign X would always represent sound A.

The Egyptians developed three different kinds of script. The first, hieroglyphic, meant "sacred carving" because it was used

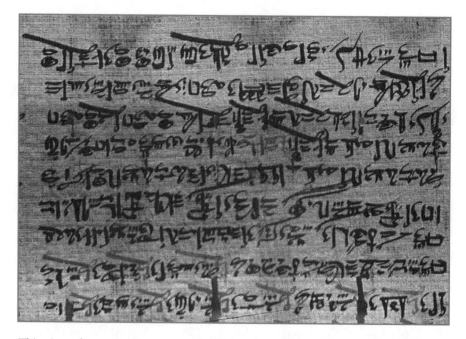

This piece of a papyrus is an example of hieratic writing, which was often used by priests for religious texts.

mostly for inscriptions on temple walls and tombs. Handwritten texts beginning in the second half of the third millennium used a cursive and faster form of hieroglyphics called hieratic. A second and even more rapid cursive script was known as demotic ("popular")—it was the ordinary writing used in daily life from the seventh century B.C. on. Scripts were written with reed brush and ink on papyrus, leather, pottery, or limestone ostraca.

Egyptian writing, like Hebrew and Arabic, normally did not indicate the vowels. Eventually, the Egyptians evolved an alphabet of twenty-four letters, for the twenty-four Egyptian consonants. But many signs represented two or three consonants. The absence of written vowels makes it impossible for us to pronounce, but that is due to our lack of knowledge of the way the Egyptians vocalized their language. Hieroglyphic can be written from left to right, right to left, or top to bottom. Hieratic and demotic always run from right to left.

Scribes were ranked according to the increasingly specialized nature of their duties. Not only writing was valued, but so was the ability to calculate. Scribes were responsible for keeping the economy going—recording income, sorting out produce, and redistributing resources. Some scribes worked as officials or priests. Scribes also interpreted the sculpted word for the majority of the people, who could neither read nor write.

As time went on, texts were produced by scribes that were not limited to economic or religious concerns. Some were created simply for pleasure, a trend encouraged by royalty. Egyptian writers produced many narratives of great interest and value. The titles alone were intriguing, including *The Man Who Was Weary of Life*; *The Tale of the Eloquent Peasant*; and *The Story of the Shipwrecked Sailor*. One of the most popular, *The Tale of Sinuhe*, some ten pages long in modern printed translation, is considered the first short story in the history of world literature.

These stories were passed on from generation to generation, lasting for centuries in the collective memory. But much of this literature was lost. One story, for instance, has been found in some four hundred copies, but none of them are complete. The names of many great authors of the past are known and, in a few cases, can be linked to an actual surviving composition. Some of these writings handed down rules of conduct meant to instruct the young in the art of getting ahead. To achieve success, the young needed to please their superiors and treat their inferiors well, according to the ancient Egyptians.

Scribes worked on projects based on their skills. The top ranking scribes were masters of hieroglyphic writing, able to convey the message of the gods and the king. Scribes of lesser rank, who knew only the cursive non-pictorial hieratic, were given administrative jobs. By the Middle Kingdom, a veritable army of scribes worked in civil service. They were the core of a rising middle class.

The art of writing was a highly specialized skill known to

This sculpture depicts an Egyptian scribe.

relatively few, and mastery of hieroglyphic signs required many years of training. But as the number of texts multiplied, the subjects of the texts became more diverse. Manuals appeared on medicine, astronomy, geometry, theology, and other topics, and there were illustrated texts of maps and games, too.

Scribes were rated higher than artisans in the social order. Artisans learned while they worked. Scribes, on the other hand, went to school to develop their skills. In fact, scribal training was the only kind of education carried on in schools.

Because it was so hard to master the writing system, training didn't begin at a very early age. Egyptian boys chosen for scribal work by their parents were sent to a government school at the age of ten. The students did much copying in hieratic script, using ostraca as notebooks, or wooden tablets that could be scraped or washed clean. Papyrus was too expensive for classroom use. Students memorized what they copied, and wrote it down again to be checked by the teacher. A repertoire of about nine hundred signs was taught. Discipline was strict. Good work was praised, and those good students were assured of an easy future and freedom from forced hard labor on public works. The lazy or incompetent student faced the possibility of physical punishment.

After finishing school, the teenager was apprenticed to a professional scribe, who was often his father or a close relative. However, the bright son of peasants or laborers might be picked out and educated. The apprentice studied the forms of documents and the methods of good administration. Learning how to write a good letter was a basic exercise. There were models offered for a variety of purposes. The letters that have survived are many, and are often enjoyable to read. They pass from royal palace to provincial governor, from father to son, nobleman to estate manager, and government department to government department. The most intimate come from family archives. Looking at Egyptian family life as it was lived thousands of years ago makes you realize how little human nature has changed.

As the scribes grew in number, they became a bureaucracy, controlling taxation and allocation of resources, of workers' pay, and of domestic and foreign trade. When you look at

Scribes help keep track of the year's grain harvest.

pictures on monuments showing economic life, there's always a highly visible scribe keeping a record of what's going on.

Because they were so important to the pharaoh's administration, scribes were highly respected and privileged. Eager to keep their status, they made no effort to simplify hieroglyphic art. That would have encouraged too many others to join in and compete. But times always change in history, even if slowly as in Egypt. Pressed by necessity, the leadership felt a wider segment of the population should be taught to read and write. In the period from about 2100 B.C. to about 1400 B.C., the number of pictographic signs was reduced to about seven hundred commonly used hieroglyphs.

The temples and palaces collected papyrus scrolls to build libraries. The aim was not to distribute the books, but simply to preserve them. Private people also collected manuscripts for their own library. The wealthy sometimes took them to their graves. These "Coffin Texts" were used to decorate the interiors of mummy cases. Maybe in the hereafter the dead could be comforted by them, or guided by them. The texts that have been found were not only religious in nature; some were literary, such as the story of *The Shepherd Who Saw a Goddess*. In the intact tomb of one artisan and his family, archaeologists made an unusual discovery—a giant ostracon was found, containing most of *The Tale of Sinuhe*.

A scribe's most valued material was papyrus. It could be rolled without cracks, and washed without damage. With ink and pen, a scribe could draw beautiful hieroglyphs, but hieratic and demotic writings were far more common on papyrus. The papyrus was made from stalks of the plant growing on the banks of the Nile. Some rose 16 feet (5 m) high. They were usually cut into 16-inch (41-cm) lengths, which determined the height of the written page. When properly prepared, all trace of moisture was eliminated and the sheet was smooth, white, and supple. Sheets were glued together to make rolls of papyrus. Medium-sized rolls would be some 20 sheets, each 16 by 16 inches (41 by 41 cm). Thus the Egyptians invented the book, as well as the material on which it was written and the script itself.

A papyrus roll now in the British Museum is 133 feet (41 m) long by 16 1/2 inches (42 cm) high. It contains 117 columns of hieratic writing. It belonged to the records of a great temple during the time of Rameses III. Another papyrus, in the Oriental Institute, Chicago, is about 167 feet (51 m) long.

The invention of papyrus was more important to the world than the invention of hieroglyphics. It was cheaper than the skin from which parchment, a much later invention, was made, and more convenient than clay tablets or slates of stone. It remained the best material for correspondence and records for centuries until paper—invented by the Chinese around A.D. 105—made its way to the Middle East.

Pictures of scribes show them always working on a mat, sitting or squatting, with the papyrus roll on their knees. The scribes wrote on both sides of the sheet. Black ink was most often used, with red ink kept for title or chapter heads, the first word of a phrase, or verse points. The Egyptians also wrote on leather and linen. No pictures show women writing, though it seems some women could read. We do know of one woman scribe, however.

THE ROSETTA STONE: A MYSTERY SOLVED

It seems strange to think that the writing of the oldest civilization in history would one day be forgotten, and that fourteen centuries would pass before someone figured out how to read hieroglyphics. After the Muslim invaders took over Egypt in the seventh century A.D., few travelers ever visited the country, and none brought back any new information of value.

The study of Egypt was dead until Napoleon and his army conquered the country in 1798. He reached Egypt with more than 150 experts, including scientists, engineers, chemists, botanists, zoologists, mineralogists, and linguists, to investigate Egypt scientifically.

In July 1799, as the French army was building fortifications near the town of Rosetta in the Nile Delta region, they dug up a black basalt stone that seemed quite unusual because three different styles of writing were carved into its surface. Army officers wondered if the stone might have special significance. Did the three forms of writing say the same thing? Wouldn't knowledge of one language provide clues to the unknown features of the other two?

Napoleon had printers pull proof copies by inking the stone, placing paper on it, and rubbing. The clear impressions that came out were sent to scholars in various parts of Europe for study. While they were examining the Rosetta Stone, the French lost Egypt to British forces and the stone itself passed to the victor. In 1802, the stone was brought to the British Museum in London, where visitors can see it today.

The stone is inscribed in three scripts—hieroglyphic, demotic, and Greek—but only two languages (ancient Egyptian and Greek). The stone is large—45 inches (114 cm) high, 28 1/2 inches (72 cm) wide, and 11 inches (28 cm) thick.

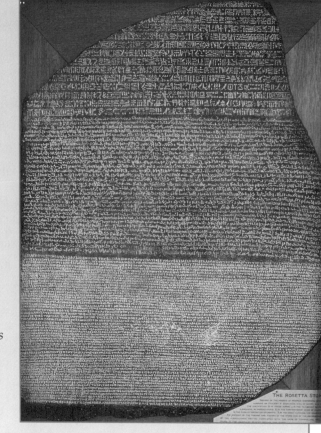

The Rosetta Stone is written in three different writing styles. On the top is the hieroglyphic text, then the hieratic text, and the Greek text is at the bottom.

However, this is only a part of a bigger piece, perhaps 5 or 6 feet high. The missing parts have never been found. Most of the Greek text and some of the demotic were preserved, but a large part of the hieroglyphic writing was missing. So when the scholars tried to translate the stone's message and decipher the languages, they worked mainly from the demotic and Greek passages.

The Greek text was translated quite quickly. A Swede and an Englishman worked on the demotic writing. The progress they made was brought to fruition by a French scholar, Jean François Champollion (1790–1832), who had been working independently to decipher the stone. A brilliant young school-master, Champollion had believed from youth that it was his destiny to solve the problem. By the time he was thirteen, he had mastered several languages. Comparing inscriptions found on an obelisk and on bas-reliefs with those on the stone, he discovered the key to the problem and published his findings in 1822 and 1824. From then on, scholars could decipher the documents archaeologists found anywhere in Egypt, and the discipline of Egyptology was launched.

What the Rosetta Stone contained was a decree passed on March 27, 196 B.C., by Egyptian priests gathered at Memphis to celebrate the first anniversary of the coronation of Ptolemy V, one of the Greek pharaohs of Macedonian descent who had begun to rule over Egypt from 205 B.C.

This sculpture depicts an ancient Egyptian family.

CHAPTER ELEVEN

FOOD, FUN, AND FAMILY

Egyptian painting and sculpture portray family groups as very loving. Children were seen as a great blessing and parents were both proud of them and generous to them. Even the poorest people welcomed all the children born to them. And the number of children born was high, averaging four to six per family; some had ten or even fifteen kids. In paintings and sculpture, the family is seen in many aspects of daily living—at work, at feasts and festivals, playing, hunting, and fishing.

Food has always been an important part of family life. But in a country like Egypt, where famine was never forgotten, food was especially valued. If the Nile floods were too slight or too violent, the harvest was bad. During invasions, food was stolen or destroyed by the enemy. Bandits burned the land, and robbed and killed the peasants. They also frightened the peasants into hiding the harvest. At such times, the peasants would sell food only for gold. In normal periods, however, there was plenty to eat. One papyrus describes the offerings made by a pharaoh to the gods, which included foodstuffs as well as precious metals, garments, and perfumes.

The Egyptians ate a great deal of meat. They fattened cattle and oxen to the point where the beasts could barely walk. The oryx, gazelle, and antelope were also important sources of food. Some farmers raised pigs, goats, and sheep. Birds, including pigeons, geese, ducks, and quails, were eaten on a large scale. Most people ate fish too, and the people of the Nile Delta and the Fayyum Lake made their living by supplying that food. Fish that reached the family table included mullet, catfish, and perch. Vegetables were also a part of the Egyptian diet and included onions, leeks, radishes, garlic, and cucumbers. The Egyptians believed that lettuce made men amorous and women fertile so they ate large amounts of it. The Egyptians enjoyed eating beans too, such as chickpeas. Their favorite fruits included grapes, figs, dates, pomegranates, olives, and apples. Not until the Roman period were pears, peaches, and cherries grown. Milk was a great delicacy, as were its by-products—cream, butter, and cheese.

In the home, people cooked with movable cylindrical earthenware stoves about 3 feet (1 m) high. The stoves had a grill or bars inside to support the fire and an opening at the bottom to allow a draft and for removal of ashes. Egypt had no coal nor did any of countries nearby. So the cooks—and anyone whose craft required the use of furnaces—had to get by with charcoal or wood.

Kitchens were equipped with saucepans, basins, and jars, all made of earthenware. The kitchen chores were done on three-legged or four-legged tables. No Egyptian cookbooks have been found, but medical papyri dealing with illnesses and indigestion indicate how foods were probably prepared.

Egyptians enjoyed a rich variety of breads and cakes, most of them containing honey, milk, fruit, eggs, fat, or butter. Barley and wheat were used to make flour. The rich had their own staff for baking but the millers and bakers set up shop to sell their wares to the poor.

Beer was Egypt's national drink. The people drank it every-where—at home, in taverns, outdoors, and aboard ships. It was made from barley or wheat and dates. The Egyptians also had wine, made from grapes grown in the Nile Delta region's many vineyards.

These were the main foods Egyptians ate throughout the year. There is little evidence of how families dined. It seems that they ate singly or in pairs, seated at small tables. Breakfast was not a family get-together. People ate separately when they got up. The other two meals were the main ones each day. The meat, vegetables, fruit in season, breads, and cakes were washed down with beer. There were lots of pottery vessels for serving the food as well as knives, spoons, and forks.

When night came, houses were lit by lamps burning either castor oil or olive oil. Family life in the evening was not long, for Egyptians usually rose at daybreak and went early to bed.

Music was always popular with Egyptians. Even before instruments were invented, they enjoyed listening to singers and accompanying them by clapping hands. By the time the pyramids were being built, the flute, oboe, and harp were in common use, played in duets or trios. Gradually, percussion instruments—castanets and tambourines—were added. At upper-class dinner parties or banquets, the guests were entertained with music and dancing.

At home, people passed the time sitting outdoors, boating on a lake, or fishing. Married couples liked to play board

A couple listens to a musician play a harp.

A toy horse and a doll are just a few examples of the toys of ancient Egyptian children.

games; some governed by throwing dice. Children had their own forms of entertainment. Children had toys and played games a bit like those of today. Rattles soothed babies, older kids liked tops and played games with balls made of wood or leather. Boys battled with toy weapons and girls played with rag dolls or wooden dolls and had tiny beds to put them in. Outside, boys might team up on opposite sides and play games that challenged their strength. Sometimes they ran obstacle races, or competed in hurling javelins at a target. Boys liked to wrestle, one on one, or in teams. Girls wrestled too, but their favorite pastime was dancing.

Women had many privileges in ancient Egypt, especially women of the upper classes and female members of royalty, such as the ancient Egyptian princess shown here.

CHAPTER TWELVE

WOMEN'S ROLES

The evidence tells us that women in ancient Egypt were respected and treated with dignity. They seem to have had a degree of independence not found in women of other ancient societies. They look beautiful and charming in many of the paintings and sculptures. The pharaohs and their wives, and other noble couples, are depicted with a warmth and intimacy unusual in the art of the Near East.

The pharaoh's women enjoyed a degree of freedom. In addition to the women of the royal court, mothers of the upper classes also had some freedom. Such women were mistresses of their houses. Their property was at their own disposal and they could will it to their children. It was they who chose the children's names, giving them their identity. And they could educate their daughters by hiring a tutor, since schools run by the government and the priesthood were strictly for boys.

Women of the upper classes did not have to worry about housework. They had slaves, often male, to do the chores. By the time of the New Kingdom, male slaves did the laundering,

A peasant woman kneads bread—only one of the many tasks women had perform to survive.

weaving, and cooking. But the hardest task, grinding grain by hand every day, was done by women slaves.

Only a precious few women led a life of ease, however. Most women were peasants whose daily lives revolved around survival. They cleaned, cooked, washed clothes, collected fuel, fetched water, went to market, and helped in the fields, especially at harvest time. Peasant women were stuck in an unending cycle of labor, interrupted only briefly to bear children. Sometimes a peasant woman's son would "make good," rise above his class, and help ease the life of his parents.

Despite social and economic class differences, the pharaoh, as chief lawgiver, viewed both male and female, and noble and peasant as equal under the law. There are other signs that women enjoyed some of the same freedoms as men. Documents show women making bargains, figuring accounts, drawing up petitions, lending money, and selling land, just as men did.

Women held important jobs, albeit not always the most high-ranking positions. In public life, women were largely absent. This may have been because male officeholders often handed on their jobs to sons. Some women, however, held positions of trust as treasurers or supervisors. Documents record women supervising a dining hall, a wig shop, professional singers, a workshop of weavers, and a royal harem. However, some positions in the civil or public service were off-limits to women. To be a king's scribe, an army general, the governor of a city or province, or an ambassador to foreign lands was impossible for women.

At first, women were the ones that did all of the weaving in ancient Egypt.

Women ran one segment of the artisan trade for a time. Prior to the New Kingdom, the textile industry seems to have been in women's hands. Women held the full range of jobs, from weavers to supervisors. Several professions were open to women—the priesthood, to a very limited degree, midwifery, mourning, dancing, and music. And there is some evidence that prostitution was not uncommon.

Marriage was a private act in ancient Egypt, with no legal

framework. Most marriages seem to have been arranged. The choice of spouse was usually made by the parents. They would choose someone from the same social class as themselves. This was believed to be the best match. Marriages sometimes took place between cousins, and even between uncle and niece. Both men and women thought marriage highly desirable. It happened at quite an early age in ancient Egypt—often at age fifteen for boys and twelve for girls. (Remember that the average life span in that ancient time was only thirty.)

The choice for most women—either to stay in their parents' home or leave it only for marriage—made early marriage attractive to them. Besides escaping the confines of their childhood home, women got married to have children. A woman's children would help her in the afterlife by saying prayers at her death and being responsible for her burial.

By marrying, a woman did not lose control of her property. A married woman had the same rights to own, inherit, and dispose of property as an unmarried woman, and anything she owned didn't pass automatically into the hands of her husband on marriage. Also, since there were no family names back then, a woman didn't change her name when she married.

Similar to most modern societies, an ancient Egyptian woman would expect to be her husband's only wife. However, this was not always the case. Polygamy—having several wives—was not unknown. To continue their dynasties, kings often had many wives so that they might have several heirs. But a commoner, even if married, could have as many concubines as he could afford and could force his wife to accept. In

This stela shows a married couple.

general, however, wives were treated with respect by husbands, families, and servants.

If a marriage was unhappy, divorce was possible in ancient Egypt. Either husband or wife could initiate a divorce. But it was a private matter between the couple, and the state had no role in it. Once divorced, both man and woman could remarry whenever they chose. And many did so.

WOMEN WHO RULED

Only a few of the country's hundreds of pharaohs were women. From the beginning of Egyptian history, the ruler was believed to be divine—the earthly embodiment of the male god Horus. However, a few women with powerful beliefs in their ability to rule did not let ritual or custom stand in their way.

Nitocris was the first woman to rule (c. 2180 B.C.). Almost nothing is known of her except that she took the throne upon the death of King Pepi II. About three years after her own death, the Old Kingdom ended.

Around four hundred years later (1790 B.C.), Queen Sobeknefru became pharaoh. She had been co-regent with her father. Upon his death she ruled alone, at the peak of the Middle Kingdom; she died three years later.

The third woman to rule, Queen Hatshepsut, left a much greater record of achievement. She became queen in 1490 B.C. during the New Kingdom. She took the throne by a daring

Queen Hatshepsut was the woman who reigned the longest as pharaoh.

move. She was the daughter of one king and the wife of another. When her husband died, his son Thutmose III, born of a minor wife, became king. But he was only a child, so Hatshepsut became his co-regent. With the backing of strong political figures and priests, she took all power and simply set the boy aside.

Hatshepsut was a good administrator and her reign brought prosperity. Rather than try to lead armies in battle, she chose peaceful pursuits. She built new monuments and obelisks, worked out a stable foreign policy, sent trading missions abroad, and to ensure her own happy afterlife, built one of the most unusual and beautiful temples on the west bank at Luxor.

Suddenly, Hatshepsut changed her royal title from "Queen" to "King." She had herself portrayed in statues and paintings in full male dress with a false beard. She governed Egypt for at least twenty-one years and died in 1483 B.C. Thutmose III then became sole ruler and turned out to be the greatest military leader Egypt had ever seen. Nearly twenty years after Hatshepsut's death, Thutmose had her name and images obliterated.

More than 1,400 years later came Cleopatra VII, the most famous of the Ptolemies. She ruled Egypt after Alexander the Great added the country to his empire. A great many poems, plays, novels, biographies, and movies have been created about this legendary ruler. Some describe her as the wickedest woman in history. Others depicted her as a faithful lover who died for her man. Still others depict her as a selfish tyrant, or as a child who never grew up.

Few of these stories about Cleopatra are based on hard fact, since scant evidence survives from two thousand years ago, when she left the stage of history. But the evidence we do have indicates that Cleopatra was a woman of powerful ambition, with the keen intelligence, charm, and political skills to make a great mark on history.

Through the centuries, there have been many stories written about Cleopatra VII, but few facts about her are known today.

Born in 69 B.C., she became queen at eighteen. At twenty-one, she became the lover of Julius Caesar, Rome's great ruler. After Caesar's assassination, she fell in love with Mark Antony, the Roman general. During the struggle for power among the leading men of Rome, she was captured in 30 B.C. by Octavian, Antony's rival, and killed herself.

She is believed to have been an accomplished scholar, a master of several languages, and a benevolent ruler who commissioned many of the great engineering projects that advanced Egypt's economy and prosperity.

TIMELINE

Era	Dynasties	Years
Early Dynastic Period	First to Third Dynasties	3100 to 2630 B.C.
Old Kingdom	Fourth to Eighth Dynasties	2630 to 2213 B.C.
First Intermediate Period	Ninth to Eleventh Dynasties	2200 to 2060 B.C.
Middle Kingdom	Twelfth to Thirteenth Dynasties	2061 to 1640 B.C.
Second Intermediate Period	Fourteenth to Seventeenth Dynasties	1640 to 1550 B.C.
New Kingdom	Eighteenth to Twentieth Dynasties	1550 to 1070 B.C.
Third Intermediate Period	Twenty-first to Twenty-fourth Dynasties	1070 to 1712 B.C.

BIBLIOGRAPHY

Andreu, Guillemette. *Egypt in the Age of the Pyramids*. Ithaca: Cornell, 1997.

Boorstin, Daniel J. *The Creators*. New York: Random House, 1992.

Boorstin, Daniel J. *The Discoverers*. New York: Random House, 1983.

Bowman, Alan K. *Egypt After the Pharaohs*. Berkeley: University of California Press, 1986.

Brier, Bob. *Egyptian Mummies*. New York: Morrow, 1994.

Brier, Bob. *The Murder of Tutankhamen*. New York: Berkeley, 1999.

Burke, James and Robert Ornstein. *The Axemaker's Gift: A Double-Edged History of Human Culture*. New York: Grosset, 1995.

Carter, Howard and A. C. Mace. *The Discovery of the Tomb of Tutankhamen*. New York: Dover, 1977.

Davidson, Basil. *African Civilization Revisited: From Antiquity to Modern Times*. Trenton: Africa World Press, 1991.

Diamond, Jared. *Guns, Germs and Steel: The Fates of Human Societies*. New York: Norton, 1997.

Donadoni, Sergio, ed. *The Egyptians*. Chicago: University of Chicago Press, 1997.

Empereur, Jean-Yves. *Alexandria Rediscovered*. New York: Braziller, 1998.

Fagan, Brian M., ed. *The Oxford Companion to Archeology*. New York: Oxford, 1996.

Finley, M. I. *The Use and Abuse of History*. New York: Penguin, 1987.

Forty, Jo. *Ancient Egyptian Pharaohs*. North Dighton, Mass.: JG Press, 1998.

Grant, Michael. *Cleopatra*. New York: Barnes & Noble, 1972.

Hart, George. *Ancient Egypt*. New York: Knopf, 1990.

Hughes-Hallett, Lucy. *Cleopatra: Histories, Dreams and Distortions*. New York: Harper & Row, 1990.

Lefkowitz, Mary. *Not Out of Africa*. New York: Basic, 1997.

Levine, Robert. *A Geography of Time*. New York: Basic, 1997.

Manguel, Alberto. *A History of Reading*. New York: Viking, 1996.

Matz, Helen C., ed. *Egypt: A Country Study*. Washington: Library of Congress, 1991.

Montet, Pierre. *Everyday Life in Egypt: In the Days of Rameses the Great*. Philadelphia: University of Pennsylvania, 1981.

Murnane, William J. *The Penguin Guide to Ancient Egypt*. New York: Penguin, 1996.

Redford, Donald B. *The Oxford Encyclopedia of Ancient Egypt*. New York: Oxford University Press, 2001.

Robins, Gay. *Women in Ancient Egypt*. Cambridge: Harvard, 1993.

Scott, Joseph and Lenore Scott. *Egyptian Hieroglyphics for Everyone: An Introduction to the Writing of Ancient Egypt*. New York: Barnes & Noble, 1993.

Shaw, Ian, ed. *The Oxford History of Ancient Egypt*. New York: Oxford University Press, 2000.

Stead, Miriam. *Egyptian Life*. Cambridge: Harvard, 1986.

Stierlin, Henri. *The Pharaohs: Master-Builders*. Paris: Terrail, 1992.

Tyldesley, Joyce. *Nefertiti: Egypt's Sun Queen*. New York: Viking, 1999.

Watterson, Barbara. *Women in Ancient Egypt*. London: Wrens Park, 1991.

Whitrow, G. J. *Time in History*. New York: Oxford, 1989.

FOR MORE INFORMATION

Books

Green, Roger Lancelyn. *Tales of Ancient Egypt*. New York: Puffin Classics, 1996.

Heinrichs, Ann. *Egypt*. Danbury, CT: Children's Press, 1997.

Payne, Elizabeth. *Pharaohs of Ancient Egypt*. New York: Random House, 1998.

Organizations and Online Sites

The Brooklyn Museum of Art
200 Eastern Parkway
Brooklyn, NY 11238
http://www.brooklynart.org

This museum has more than five hundred objects from ancient Egypt in its collection, including a portion of a vizier's tomb from the eighth century B.C.

The Cleveland Museum of Art
University Circle
11150 East Boulevard
Cleveland, OH 44106-1797
http://www.clemusart.com
View highlights of the museum's Egyptian collection on its online site.

The Detroit Institute of Arts
5200 Woodward Avenue
Detroit, MI 48202
http://www.dia.org
This museum has many items from ancient Egypt in its collection, and several sculptures from ancient Egypt can be seen on its online site.

Giza
http://www.memst.edu/egypt/giza.htm
See the pyramids of Giza at this online site by the University of Memphis.

Kelsey Museum of Archeology
University of Michigan
434 South State Street

Ann Arbor, MI 48109

http://www.umich.edu/~kelseydb/

This museum's collection includes artifacts from ancient Egypt and the Near East as well as Greek and Roman works.

Los Angeles County Museum of Art

5905 Wilshire Boulevard

Los Angeles, CA 90036

http://www.lacma.org

This museum has approximately two thousand works of art from ancient Egypt. Its online site offers visitors a glimpse of some of the artifacts accompanied by an explanation.

The Metropolitan Museum of Art

1000 Fifth Avenue

New York, NY 10028

http://www.metmuseum.org

Explore ancient Egypt through this museum's extensive collection. Its online site includes many artifacts, and even has a special section called "Egyptian Art in the Age of the Pyramids."

Museum of Fine Arts

Avenue of the Arts

465 Huntington Avenue

Boston, MA 02115-5523

http://www.mfa.org

The museum offers a special section on its online site called

"Pharaohs of the Sun" where visitors can learn more about ancient Egypt.

The Newark Museum
49 Washington Street
P.O. Box 540
Newark, NJ 07101-0540
http://www.newarkmuseum.org
This museum's classical collection includes many objects from ancient Egypt.

The Oriental Institute
1155 East 58th Street
Chicago, IL 60637
http://www-oi.uchicago.edu/OI/default.html
Through its online site, the museum offers a virtual museum, images of its Egyptian collection, and recommended books for students.

Phoebe A. Hearst Museum of Anthropology
103 Kroeber Hall
University of California
Berkeley, CA 94720
http://www.qal.berkeley.edu/~hearst/
This museum has more than twenty thousand objects from ancient Egypt in its collection, including pottery, tools, jewelry, clothing, and other artifacts.

University of Pennsylvania Museum of Archaeology and Anthropology

Thirty-third and Spruce Streets

Philadelphia, PA 19104

http://www.upenn.edu/museum/index.html

This museum's online site provides information on ancient Egyptian culture, and includes fun activities, such as how to write your name in hieroglyphics.

The Walters Art Museum

600 North Charles Street

Baltimore, MD 21201

http://www.thewalters.org

This museum contains many works from ancient Egypt in its ancient art collection.

INDEX

ABOUT THE AUTHOR

Milton Meltzer has written nearly one hundred books for young people and adults in the fields of history, biography, and social reform. He has also dealt with such diverse topics as memory, names, gold, the potato, the horse, food, and altruism. He has written or edited for newspapers, magazines, books, radio, television, and films.

Among the many honors for his books are five nominations for the National Book Award, as well as the Christopher, Jane Addams, Carter G. Woodson, Regina Medal, Jefferson Cup, Washington Book Guild, Olive Branch, and Golden Kite awards. He was the 2001 Laura Ingalls Wilder award winner, honoring him for his "substantial and lasting contribution" to children's literature. Many of his books have been chosen for the honor lists of the American Library Association, the National Council of Teachers of English, and the National Council for the Social Studies, as well as *The New York Times* Best Books of the Year list.

Meltzer and his wife, Hildy, live in New York. They have two daughters, Jane and Amy, and two grandsons, Benjamin and Zachary. Mr. Meltzer is a member of the Authors Guild, American PEN, and the Organization of American Historians.